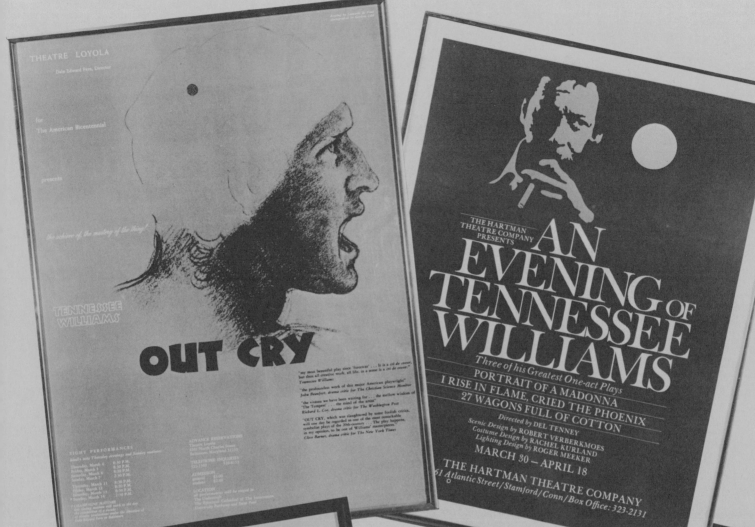

THE WORLD OF TENNESSEE WILLIAMS

THE WORLD OF TENNESSEE WILLIAMS

Edited by Richard F. Leavitt

With an introduction by
Tennessee Williams

G. P. Putnam's Sons, New York

To George Robison Black
and *A la Recherche du Temps Perdu*

Designed by Emilio Squeglio and Rick Celano

Copyright © 1978 by Richard F. Leavitt
All rights reserved. This book, or parts
thereof, must not be reproduced in any form
without permission. Published simultaneously
in Canada by Longman Canada Limited, Toronto, Canada
SBN: 399-11773-3
Library of Congress Cataloging in Publication Data

Leavitt, Richard F
  The world of Tennessee Williams.

Includes index.
  1. Williams, Tennessee, 1911- 2. Dramatists,
American—20th century—Biography.   I. Williams,
Tennessee, 1911- II. Title.
PS3545.I5365Z735   812′.5′4 [B]   76-28473

PRINTED IN THE UNITED STATES OF AMERICA

Editor's Note and Acknowledgments

Since this is a pictorial approach to the world of Tennessee Williams, it has seemed unnecessary to encumber it with footnotes or with other literary apparatus.

The primary source for most of the commentary in this book has been, of course, Tennessee Williams himself—what he has told me directly or what I have observed firsthand. In all other instances, remarks or quotes attributed to him have been taken directly from his collected private papers or other published letters, and from books and interviews about him.

In addition to that vast and ever-growing mountain of critical "literature" (a book a month, at last count) concerning his life and his work, my secondary sources include my own conversations and correspondence with mutual personal friends who have substantiated and often clarified for me what time has dimmed.

I am aware of certain discrepancies with other published accounts concerning the circumstances of the whereabouts of Williams at various times throughout his life, but I have chosen to let the record stand as I have reconstructed it. I find the published variations in themselves interesting.

I have resisted any temptation to analyze his work and have attempted only such general comment as I have felt qualified to make, and which seemed natural and appropriate to enhance the pictorial content of the book.

All illustrations unless otherwise credited are from the Williams collection at the Humanities Research Center, the University of Texas at Austin. I spent two rewarding weeks at that handsome facility, and for the many courtesies I received there I would like to thank Dr. David Farmer, John R. Payne, Lois Garcia, Linda Hodges, and especially "Mrs. Mac"—May Ellen MacNamara. Jane Combs and her assistant Dave Schaefer were most helpful with the Downing Collection in the Hoblitzelle Theatre Arts Library.

Acknowledgment is made to reprint from "The Broken Tower" by Hart Crane the lines which appear under the title "Southern Gothic." Reprinted from *The Complete Poems and Selected Letters and Prose of Hart Crane,* Edited by Brom Weber. By permission of Liveright Publishing Corporation. Copyright 1938, (c) 1958, 1966 by Liveright Publishing Corporation.

I am most grateful to actor-producer-director Hume Cronyn for his arduous search in locating the series of notes exchanged by Jessica Tandy and Tennessee Williams during the New York run of *Streetcar.*

Likewise I am grateful to the many people who called or corresponded with me in connection with this book. They include Rodney Erickson, Dakin Williams, Paul Bigelow, Jordan Massee, Gilbert Maxwell, Paul Bowles, Robert A. Morgan, Jr., Peter Harvey, Owen Phillips, Ruth Brinkman, Evelyn Lawson,

Christopher Isherwood, Norma Nannini, Owen D. Nee, Phyllis Malinow, and Clark Mills.

Reference librarians throughout the country have been unfailingly helpful, but I would especially like to thank Ada M. Stoflet of the University of Iowa and Mr. Louis A. Rachow, librarian of the Walter Hampden Memorial Library at the Players Club, both of whom went far beyond the normal courtesies and provided me with exceptional, hard-to-find material for which I am most grateful.

I wish to thank Key West photographers Wright and Joan Langley and Don Pinder for their quick service and hours of research. Several of the best production stills in this book were taken by Joseph Abeles, one of the deans of Broadway photographers, and getting to know him has been one of the great rewards of this book.

I am grateful to Andreas Brown, president of The Gotham Book Mart and Gallery in New York City, not only for the initial introduction to Bill Targ, but for his continued interest and helpful assistance with the bibliography.

Bob and Joan Chase know they have my thanks, as do Bob and Linda Shaw. I am indebted to Putnam's Senior Editor Bill Targ and to Tennessee's agent, Bill Barnes, for their encouragement and patience during the preparation of the manuscript.

I very much appreciate the loan of an extensive number of rare photographs from the private collection of George Robison Black, and I want to thank poet Frederick Nicklaus for reading the manuscript and making so many excellent suggestions.

Finally, of course, I would like to thank Tennessee Williams for allowing me to rummage through his life in Key West, New Orleans, Miami, and New York at times when he had more important things to do.

R.F.L.
Colebrook, New Hampshire

Contents

Introduction

"At the Expense of the Future"

Over lunch at La Côte Basque in New York one noon last spring, I happily and rashly committed myself to a professional undertaking which this midsummer daybreak in my Key West studio finds me somewhat regretting as I have sometimes regretted impulsive commitments of this nature in the past, influenced by noon wine in genial company.

Here I am faced with a commitment: writing a preface to a book of photographs and other memorabilia collected by my old, though still young, friend Dick Leavitt for the publishing firm of Putnam's, which also brought out, years ago, my mother's book, *Remember Me to Tom.*

And if I seem to be spinning out words this morning, like a disoriented spider might spin out his web over a hornet's nest, it is because, now presently confronted with what was a futurity, I feel as though hoisted upon my own petard.

In the course of his professional lifetime a writer is called upon to write some things sometime that strike him as being somewhat superfluous; and this Introduction to a collection of press clippings, photos and other graphic reminders of my life, memorabilia associated with my profession, does strike me that way. Yet we have obligations, we have commitments in every walk of life.

I have now illustrated my embarrassment over this particular assignment. I would go no further were it not for the sake of Dick Leavitt,

and Putnam senior editor Bill Targ—at least I would prefer not to. Still, this undertaking on my part is small compared to my friend Dick Leavitt's long and exacting task of getting these bits and pieces of evidence together. To withhold a bit of testimony in my own defense or prosecution would be niggardly of me.

And still I sit here wondering what to say as a foreword to these mostly pictorial memoirs.

To begin with, perhaps I could insert a quote from Amanda Wingfield: "The past keeps getting bigger and bigger at the expense of the future."

When Dick Leavitt first allowed me to look over the collection, I made but one strong complaint: that it almost suggested that I had ceased to exist about 1961, while actually it was at that point that I began upon a metamorphosis as a playwright that contained points of intensity as significant to myself as those before.

It is understandable that Dick should have been swayed by general opinion, what is called the consensus. That decade of the sixties, as it concerned myself again, appeared to the great plurality of outside observers as a time more properly spelt as decayed.

"He put on fat as a widow puts on mourning" is a quote from a short story of mine. The fat that I put on was the fat of liquor and other indulgences such as physical sloth.

Then all of a sudden it was another decade, the still mysterious seventies. Apocalyptic events in my life, registering at least eight points on the Richter scale, woke me up to the fact that, being still a survivor, I'd better start concentrating on that privilege and make of it what I could while it continued.

I found two great confederates: a personal representative, Bill Barnes, who thought I should and believed I could continue—and my own new wish to, a very strong wish that could be termed obsessive.

It takes a good shaking up to change the inner gravitational field of the psyche.

Backed into a corner, that's when and where the spirit of a being must really put up a fight. Otherwise, well, it's messy. . . .

I am comforted by the thought, as I hastily wind up this "dispensable" Introduction, that by the time this book comes off the press into the bookstores, a good deal of light and shadow will be more clearly defined.

"Inordinately possessed of the past" is a striking phrase that Christopher Makos used concerning me in a recent interview. It was not only an excellent phrase but a true one of the subject. I am an avid collector of memories, yes, but not of memorabilia. Much as I have been pleased by awards, by many play posters, and even by certain notices, I don't frame them and hang them on the walls. I've usually passed these trophies on to my mother since they were not adaptable to such an itinerant kind of life as I've led.

Some years ago my friend Andreas Brown, of Manhattan's internationally famed Gotham Book Mart, researched through the old family residence in suburban Clayton, Missouri, mostly in the basement where I used to work and where a lot of finished and unfinished stories, plays, correspondence, et cetera, had been left behind me. He, and his lawyer at the time, discovered a marvelous repository for it in the archives of the Humanities Department of the University of Texas at Austin.

Much of the material in this book has been reproduced from things deposited there.

This gives me a chance to say thanks to the Humanities Department of the University of Texas, to my friend Andreas Brown, to my mother, to her own well-ordered depository in Clayton—and even to what remains of my capacity to meet all commitments.

Tennessee Williams

PART 1
Southern Gothic

1

Southern Gothic

And so it was I entered the broken world, to
trace the visionary company of love, its voice an
instant in the wind (I know not whither hurled)
but not for long to hold each desperate choice.
—HART CRANE
"The Broken Tower"

Tennessee Williams is a dramatist of lost souls. His milieu is the South, a tense and unreconstructed locale typical only of an environment we all inhabit. In the mythology of his work, the South is an antebellum mansion of faded elegance inhabited by gentle dreamers, misfits, fugitives, and outcasts—losers who are not meant to win.

Always the gothic focus of his work echoes an awareness of loneliness and loss, a sense of corruption and the physical violence which is an aspect of southern romanticism. His theme is the plight of the individual trapped by his environment, the loneliness and lack of communication between human beings unable to reconcile the flesh with the spirit. It is his special genius to temper extremes of physical violence, brutality, and perversion with gentle, loving glimpses of humanity and a passionate concern for dispossessed people living on the border line of despair.

Williams has brought to the American theater a highly poetic literary individuality. His plays are extended metaphors built on symbolic characterization to the point where their very structure is determined by the revelation of character. Plot is telegraphed by mood. Always his literary bent is toward the symbolic and the mystical, more so in his female than in his male characters. "My chief aim in playwriting is the creation of character. I have always had a deep feeling for the mystery of life, and essentially

my plays have been an effort to explore the beauty and meaning in the confusion of living."

Tennessee Williams is an old-fashioned southern romantic who never made any kind of adjustment to the real world, a world he constantly wanders in search of the sad music in people. Like the characters he stylizes—spiritualizes—out of existence, he exults in a shadowy existence above a substantial one. "All work is autobiographical if it is serious. Everything a writer produces is sort of his inner history, transposed into another time." The most subjective of writers, Williams' humor is robust, earthy, and always evident. "It is simply not in my nature as a dramatist to work without humor no matter how desperate may be the fates and situations of the protagonists."

Tennessee Williams is an electrifying scenewright; an acknowledged master of stage poetics. In creating mood, using every device of the theater—setting, lights, costumes, music—he has few equals. His lyricism gracefully accentuates the atmosphere of decay which permeates his work. And he writes to suit his severest critic—himself. Other critics have noted that he has never created a character who has recovered from the wounds and desolation of childhood. Williams is nothing if not honest. His best plays are those based on his own life.

Williams was born in the South and descends from a long line of southerners. His mother thinks he was born with his eyes wide open at a world which fascinated him. For a writer whose work would often revolve around religious holidays, the date was auspicious: March 26, 1911—Palm Sunday.

Christened Thomas Lanier III for his paternal grandfather whose notable East Tennessee family were frontiersmen and Indian fighters during pioneer days, his pride in this cavalier branch of the family would one day prompt him to take for his own the name Tennessee.

His paternal grandmother's people were early settlers of Nantucket Island; the poet Tristam Coffin was her uncle. In his paternal line was the southern poet Sidney Lanier.

In decided contrast with his father's heritage, his mother's was gentle and patrician. The Dakins could trace their ancestry back to a ship's captain who crossed the English Channel with William the Conqueror. Williams' maternal grandfather, the Reverend Walter Edwin Dakin, was an aristocratic, well-read, liberal churchman with a penchant for always moving on during his active years in the Episcopal ministry. Williams' beloved grandmother— "Grand"—was German. Her name was Rosina Maria Francesca Otte—Rose to the family—and Tennessee's only sister was named after her.

Williams' father, Cornelius Coffin Williams, was a boisterous, strong-willed man's man whose mother died in his early childhood. He was brought up mainly by his older sister, Ella Williams. He received a military school education. Prior to his promotion to a desk job with the International Shoe Company in St. Louis, he had enjoyed a salesman's life on the road with its attendant camaraderie and high good times. The loss of this free, easygoing life on the road unquestionably contributed to his family's later unhappiness.

In contrast with her cavalier husband, prim Edwina Dakin, the beautiful high-strung minister's daughter, embodied the sterner traits of a Puritan, and from the beginning, the strains in their marriage were apparent. This was destined to have a disastrous effect on young Tom and Rose.

Basic to the work of Tennessee Williams is the confusion which results from the repressiveness of southern Calvinism with its flesh-denying patterns of Puritanism on the romantic Cavaliers: flesh denied becomes flesh perverted. His enormous sense of guilt, the result of his own youthful rebellion against his mother's Puritan code, has never ceased to obsess him.

Home for young Tom Williams was a succession of Episcopal rectories in Mississippi, where his family lived with his mother's parents. His father traveled most of the time, and his loud, dreaded visits were brief. Together with his mother and his adored sister, Rose, both of whom he closely resembled, he grew up sheltered in the warm love of his Dakin grandparents. "Before I was eight, my life was completely unshadowed by fear. My sister and I were gloriously happy. We sailed paper boats in washtubs of water, cut lovely paper dolls out of huge mail-order catalogs, kept two white rabbits under the back porch, baked mud pies in the sun upon the front walk, climbed up and slid down the big woodpile, collected from neighboring alleys and trash-piles bits of colored glass that were diamonds and rubies and sapphires and emeralds. And in the evenings, when the white moonlight streamed over our bed, before we were asleep, our Negro nurse, Ozzie, as warm and black as a moonless Mississippi night, would lean above our bed, telling in a rich low voice her amazing tales about foxes and bears and rabbits and wolves that behaved like human beings."

Sometime at the age of five or six, while accompanying his grandfather on parish calls, he discovered what would later become the key to one of his most beautiful symbols: "I remember a lady named Laura Young . . . she was something green and cool in a sulphurous landscape. But there was a shadow upon her. For that reason we called upon her more frequently than anyone else. She loved me. I adored her. She lived in a white house near an orchard and in an arch between two rooms were hung some pendants of glass that were a thousand colors. That is a prism, she said. She lifted me and told me to shake them. When I did, they made a delicate music."

Following his nearly fatal attack of diphtheria with complications at the age of six, childhood's happiest years ended abruptly for Tom and Rose. As a result of his father's promotion to sales manager with the International Shoe Company, in 1918 the family moved to St. Louis. It was a traumatic move which deeply affected both children. Gone was their own backyard in spacious southern rectories, their carefree lives as the somewhat sheltered grandchildren of the Episcopal vicar, and gone too was a certain elevated social status they had accepted as completely natural. To combat the harsh experience of their father's constant presence, the malign snobbery and the ridicule they encountered for their southern ways, they turned more and more to each other, and the strong bond between them grew even stronger. They became allies in an alien world.

As a young dramatist Tennessee Williams would remember their years of living in congested neighborhoods; he would recall in particular one dark near-windowless apartment where his sister's room overlooked an areaway they dubbed "death valley." He would remember how they painted her furniture white and hung white curtains at the window to relieve the gloom of perpetual twilight in a room where the shade was always drawn against the grim sight of dead cats below. But mostly he would remember the array of little glass ornaments—animals mostly—which his sister collected on shelves around the room. By poetic association, they would come to represent all the softest emotions that belong to the remembrance of time past . . . all the small and tender things that relieve the austere pattern of life and make it endurable to the sensitive.

To ease his mother's household chores when his brother, Dakin, was born, Tom was sent to spend a year with his Dakin grandparents in Clarksdale, Mississippi. In the riches of his grandfather's classical library he discovered and devoured a world of books.

Back home in St. Louis, to escape the growing vise of anger which gripped the household with increasing frequency during his father's arguments with his wife, arguments often fueled by alcohol, the boy turned more and more to books and to the $10 typewriter his mother had given him on his eleventh birthday. Increasingly too, his sister, Rose, was finding her own escape. During adolescence she began to withdraw from a world which frightened her, a withdrawal which would result in schizophrenia, later to be permanently fixed by a lobotomy in a Missouri state asylum.

Williams has said of his sister's condition at this time that it was as if she had gone on a journey, yet remained in sight. To compensate for the growing loss of Rose from their special universe and for his own increasing loneliness and shyness, he embarked on a different journey, one that would carry him to a world of heights he never dreamed of. He began to write.

He found in writing a release and a refuge for his intense interior life, and from the beginning, writing came quite naturally to him. He became a lifelong compulsive and prolific writer. The poems and vignettes and sketches and short stories poured from his typewriter. By sixteen he had won $25 from the Pillsbury Flour Company for answering, in *Smart Set* magazine, "Can a Good Wife Be a Good Sport?" Other recognition and awards followed: for a movie review of *Stella Dallas*, for various poems and sonnets, and then, from *Weird Tales* magazine, $25 for "The Vengeance of Nitocris." He was seventeen years old, and it was his first published short story.

A tour of Europe when his grandfather escorted a group of church ladies brightened his last summer before graduation in 1929 from University City High School. He earned a B average. That fall he entered the University of Missouri, his tuition paid by his Grandmother Dakin. But that summer he spent escorting Hazel Kramer, a girl who had been his dear friend and close companion since grammar school days.

His first night at college he wrote to her and proposed marriage, but she gently turned him down, saying that they both were too young to think about it. Later, in college, he wrote poetry to another girl. Still later his first short story published under the name of "Tennessee," "The Field of Blue Children," would introduce a theme which would haunt much of his later work: the sense of two individuals searching for something in a world which does not exist, nor ever can exist for them, something that cannot ever be gained through the sexual experience.

At the University of Missouri he became the first freshman ever to win an honorable mention from the Dramatic Arts Club (a short play called *Beauty Is the Word*). He studied journalism and wrote death notices and livestock news for the school paper, *The Eliot*. (He preferred the death notices.) But his three years there were desultory and lackluster, and they ended abruptly when he failed ROTC. His father, furious at this affront to his family's military tradition, pulled him out of school, financed a quick course in typing, and started him in at the International Shoe Company as a clerk/typist.

Williams hated it. He would recall it as his season in hell. The work was monotonous and tiring: dusting hundreds of pair of shoes each morning, carrying heavy cases of them across town in the afternoon, and typing digits, endless lists of digits. What he did like was the easy camaraderie with his fellow workers, the daily exchange of talk about movies, stage shows, and radio programs. And he began writing at night, scheduling himself to one short story a week with half of Saturday and all of Sunday devoted to its completion. To overcome fatigue and sleepiness, he chain-smoked and consumed quantities of black coffee. Occasionally, at work during the day, he wrote poetry in the lids of shoe boxes. But it was all too much for him, and when he heard the depressing news that Hazel Kramer had married, he suffered a nervous attack which hospitalized him for ten days. And then he resigned from the shoe company. He was twenty-four years old.

If his years at the shoe warehouse were an indescribable torment to him as a person, they were invaluable to him as a writer. He learned firsthand what it meant to be trapped in a hopelessly routine job, and the experience left him with an abiding compassion for workers forced to submerge their souls in mechanized labor. He would never write a sympathetic word about any business employer, and when he turned twenty-one, he cast his first and last presidential ballot, for Norman Thomas. He would become a spokesman not for the oppressed class, but for the repressed individual.

To recover his health, he went to stay with his Dakin grandparents, now living in retirement in Memphis, and it was there during the summer of 1934 that Tennessee Williams and the theater found each other. A girl who lived nearby was involved in little theater, and as therapy she suggested that he write a play. Although he had yet to meet one sailor, Williams wrote a comedy about two sailors on shore leave who pick up a couple of girls, and *Cairo! Shanghai! Bombay!* was duly produced in Mrs. Roseboro's Rose Arbor Theater. (Talk about prophetic names.) It was a modest success, but he was enchanted by the loud, genuine laughter.

That fall "Grand" again scraped up the tuition, and he signed up for courses at Washington University in St. Louis. A basement cubicle in the nearby home of his friend Clark Mills became their "Literary Factory," and there the two young poets constantly wrote and read and laughed. It was an intensely stimulating time, but of even greater importance to Williams the playwright was his introduction to a dynamic little theater group called the Mummers of St. Louis who flourished during the last half of the thirties under the sure direction of Willard Holland. It is to the Mummers of St. Louis that Tennessee Williams can trace his real beginnings in the theater. They were his professional youth, and with them he found answers concerning himself and his future.

He wrote two plays for the Mummers, mostly about sad people with problems—material he knew well. If these early plays lacked unity, they also revealed many of the strengths which would later become characteristic of his work: flashes of poetic writing, realistic dialogue, memorable characterization, and several well-rounded individual scenes.

He continued to write in college, but his interests narrowed. He had outgrown fraternity life, most subjects bored him, and his grades fell. Still abnormally shy and always reticent with strangers (something he would never outgrow), he made little effort to attract new friends. When his play about a munitions manufacturer, *Me, Vaysha,* failed to win first prize in a contest, and following a disagreement with school policy, he wrote a furious letter to the dean and left Washington University. Life at home was intolerable. His father called writing a sissy occupation and constantly discouraged him. Family quarrels were depressing, and Rose was rapidly losing all touch with reality.

In a final attempt to help him finish college, "Grand" paid the tuition, and he entered the University of Iowa to study drama. While he was there and without consulting him, his parents permitted a frontal lobotomy to be performed on his sister. The operation rendered her passive but destroyed any hope for eventual recovery. He never forgave the operation, and when he graduated from college in the summer of 1938, he took bitter steps to free himself once and for all from the ambivalent ties to home. They would lead him to a whole new life.

The wistful beauty of the past is always an element in the work of Tennessee Williams. Blue is the color of distance and it is also the color of memory—a symbol of longing for the "sweet bird" of his youth in a country touched with the merciful blur of remembrance. His characters live beyond the fleeting moments of the drama, back into a glowing past of youth, purity, honor—all the ideals that have crumbled along with the family fortunes and mansions.

FROM GHOSTS ALONG THE MISSISSIPPI BY CLARENCE JOHN LAUGHLIN, COPYRIGHT 1948, 1961

"I write out of love for the South. But I can't expect southerners to realize that my writing about them is an expression of love. It is out of a regret for a South that no longer exists that I write of the forces which have destroyed it."

ANGUS MCBEAN, LONDON. COLLECTION OF TENNESSEE WILLIAMS

Sidney Lanier, America's "Sweet Singer of Songs" whose haunting musical poetry is among the best southern writing of the nineteenth century. Through the Laniers Williams descends from Valentine Xavier, the younger brother of Saint Francis Xavier, whose name Williams would take when he converted to Roman Catholicism. As a fledgling writer, Tennessee briefly called himself "Valentine Xavier" and he would use the name again in *Orpheus Descending*.

Dr. Walter Edwin Dakin was the teaching head of a private girls' school in East Tennessee when he entered the Episcopal ministry. He considered himself English Catholic and was very High Church. One of his favorite expressions was: "High and crazy, low and lazy." Williams revered his grandfather, who lived for ninety-eight years, and modeled Nonno, the world's oldest living poet in *The Night of the Iguana,* after him. Interestingly enough, Williams has never in any play depicted a minister in a sympathetic light.

Of his beloved grandmother, Rosina Maria Francesca Otte, Williams would one day write, "All that is not the worst of me surely comes from 'Grand.'" Later, in a touching memoir of her, he would further recall that "visits from 'Grand' meant nickels for ice-cream, quarters for movies, picnics at Forest Park; it meant gay and soft laughter between our mother and her mother, voices that ran up and down like finger exercises on the piano. 'Grand' was all that we knew of God in our lives."

Through her savings, earned in part from teaching piano and violin, she sacrificed unselfishly for her grandson. Her death just before his first financial success remains one of the cruel disappointments in his life.

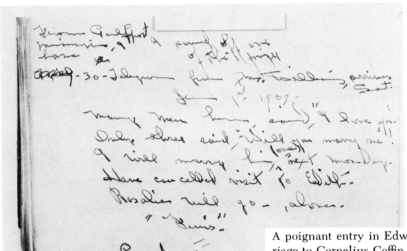

"The play is memory . . . I am the narrator of the play, also a character in it. The other characters are my mother, Amanda, my sister, Laura . . . there is a fifth character in the play who doesn't appear except in this larger-than-life photograph over the mantel. This is our father who left us a long time ago. He was a telephone man who fell in love with long distances; he gave up his job with the telephone company and skipped the light fantastic out of town. . . ."

—The Glass Menagerie

A poignant entry in Edwina's diary just before her marriage to Cornelius Coffin Williams. Their son Tom would make good use of her Gentlemen Callers.

19

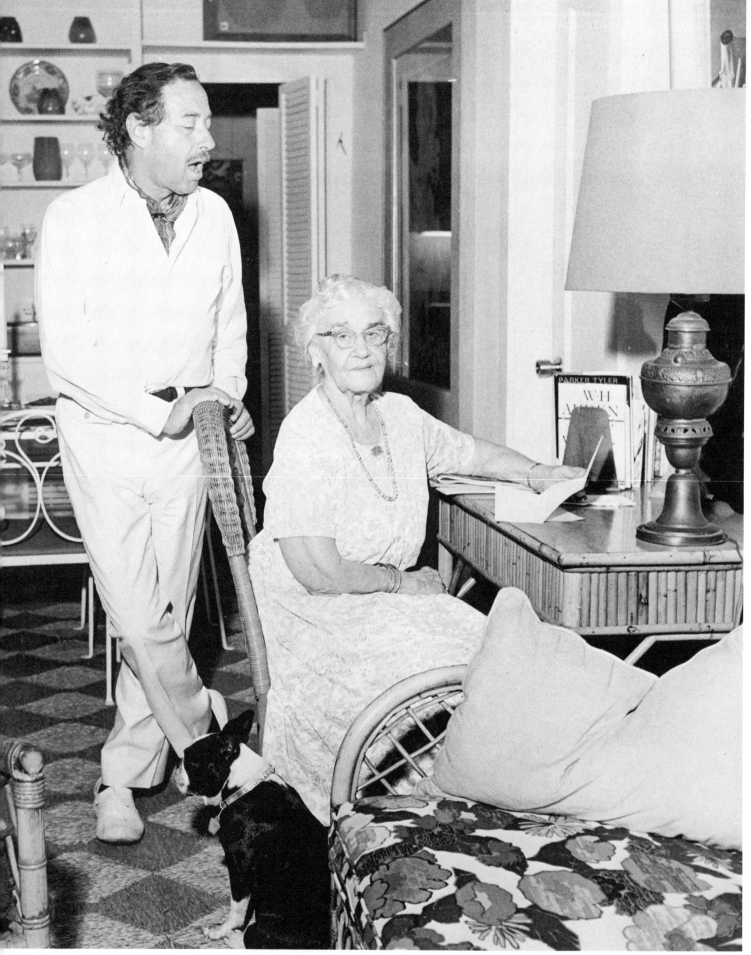

Tom and his mother in his Key West home soon after his release from Barnes Hospital in late 1969. He once asked her if she knew the meaning of "sibling rivalry." To his amazement she answered, "Yes."

WRIGHT LANGLEY

Rose Williams at the age of seventeen still shared an unusually close bond with her brother. One prominent critic of the theater has observed that the true theme of Williams' work is incest. Unsullied though it was, their love for each other was and is the deepest in their lives. Her withdrawal from the world would give him the rose as a mystical symbol of love, a symbol representing the outcast and the sensitive whose vulnerability subjects them invariably to mutiliation and destruction by a world which finds them irrelevant.

COLLECTION OF TENNESSEE WILLIAMS

Of Roses

All roses are enchantment to the wise,
the veil of sophistry drawn from the eyes,
the heart washed clean of an accustomed stain
by gusts of memory as fresh as rain.

In the confine of gardens or grown wild
they are the crystal vision of a child,
unstained by craft, undisciplined by grief,
sweet as child's laughter, and as wild and brief...

An early poem by
Thomas Lanier (Tennessee) Williams

Ironically, a school named for the children's poet Eugene Field holds bitter memories for Williams. He was tormented and teased by schoolmates for his southern accent and manners and otherwise bullied and called "sissy." Even a teacher ridiculed him. His natural shyness intensified to the point where it was agony for him to recite in class. In high school it grew to almost pathological proportions.

THE ST. LOUIS SCHOOL SYSTEM, ST. LOUIS, MISSOURI

White Star Line

On board S.S "HOMERIC"

The summer he was seventeen, Williams sailed to Europe with his Grandfather Dakin aboard the *SS Homeric*, once the pride of the Kaiser's merchant fleet. In New York's Grand Central Station he purchased *Weird Tales* magazine, which contained his first published story.

Inspired by a paragraph in a History by Heroditus, this gothic tale of revenge concerned an Egyptian queen who avenged her brother's murder by drowning his murderers in an underground chamber at the height of a festive banquet. Williams has observed, half in jest, that this story set the tone for much of his later work.

In Italy, Tom was photographed at the tomb of that country's Unknown Soldier. In Paris, the $100 spending money given him by his father was stolen by a pickpocket in the Eiffel Tower. In the Gothic cathedral of Cologne, he had a mystical religious experience which resulted in his believing that the hand of Jesus had touched his head with mercy.

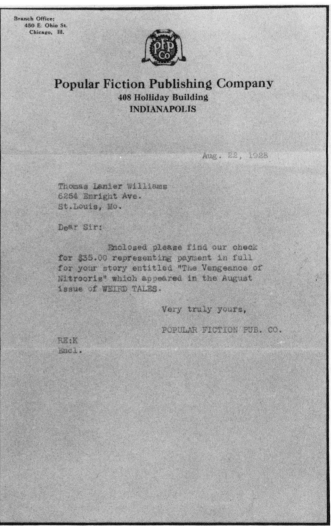

Branch Office:
450 E. Ohio St.
Chicago, Ill.

Popular Fiction Publishing Company
408 Holliday Building
INDIANAPOLIS

Aug. 22, 1928

Thomas Lanier Williams
6254 Enright Ave.
St.Louis, Mo.

Dear Sir:

Enclosed please find our check for $35.00 representing payment in full for your story entitled "The Vengeance of Nitrocris" which appeared in the August issue of WEIRD TALES.

Very truly yours,

POPULAR FICTION PUB. CO.

RE:K
Encl.

The warehouse of the International Shoe Company at Fifteenth and Delmar streets in the old downtown St. Louis was a prison to Williams during his three years' confinement there—years he would deduct from his age as years that he never really lived, thus forever confusing his biographers.

Williams wrote poetry to several different girls in college, but more than a few were written to Anna Jean O'Donnell.

Hazel Kramer and Williams had been close friends since that day in childhood when he rushed to defend her against some boys who were throwing rocks. She was a tall, auburn-haired girl with great brown eyes who let him kiss her twice a year at Christmas and on her birthday. She walked with a slight stoop to avoid appearing taller than his 5′6″. For him, their friendship ripened into love.

Williams saw Alla Nazimova as Mrs. Alving in Ibsen's *Ghosts* from the peanut gallery of the American Theatre in St. Louis during the national tour of the 1934 revival. He was profoundly impressed. "It was so moving that I had to go out and walk in the lobby during the last act. I'd stand in the door and look in, then I'd rush back to the lobby again. I suppose that play was one of the things that made me want to write for the theatre."

THE GARDEN PLAYERS

present

"CAIRO, SHANGHAI, BOMBAY"

by

BERNICE DOROTHY SHAPIRO & TOM WILLIAMS

Directed by: ARTHUR B. SCHARFF

Cast in order of first appearance:

GEORGE MADLINGER ....as THE OLD MAN
LOLE ROSEBROUGH ....as THE CHILD
MRS. HUBERT HASTINGS with   as THE MOTHER
   BABY MARY LOU HURT...........................and BABY
CATHERINE GIBSON................................as THE SPINSTER
MARY BETH CLOWER . . . . as MILLIE

DOROTHY WILSON . . . . as AILEEN

ARTHUR B. SCHARFF . . . . as UNKNOWN AUTHOR

FRED FAEHRMAN   . . . . as FAMOUS AUTHOR
HARRIETT LOOP ....at the bar
TOMMY SANDERS . . . . as CHUCK
CHESTER LOOP . . . . as HARRY

HARVEY PIERCE ....
RAYMOND HURT .... as SAILORS
HUBERT HASTINGS...............................

                    TIME: TODAY
                    PLACE: A SEAPORT TOWN

     SCENE I. A park facing harbour; early evening.

     SCENE II. A cheap Oriental Garden; 2 hours later.

     SCENE III. A backyard; few hours later.

     SCENE IV. Another part of the park, as in Scene I;
                one-half hour later.

The first playbill to bear his name. He liked the applause.

25

Thomas Williams Wins Theater Guild Contest

THOMAS WILLIAMS, '6634 Pershing avenue, University City, was awarded first prize for his play, "The Magic Tower," in the contest sponsored by the Webster Groves Theater Guild. The winners were announced at a meeting of the Guild last Tuesday. First honorable mention was given Mrs. H. C. Butler of Webster Groves for her play, "The Third Act," and Howard Buermann of St. Louis received second honorable mention for "Debt Takes a Holiday."

The three plays will be produced by the Guild in October. Judges in the contest were Miss Charity Grace, Elmore Condon and Colvin. McPherson.

Williams' initial effort for the Mummers of St. Louis was a twelve-minute antimilitary piece called *Headlines*. It was presented as a curtain raiser with Irwin Shaw's *Bury the Dead* on Armistice Day, 1936, but he received no program credit. He followed this early success with a long play called *Candle to the Sun*, a violent story about Alabama coal miners which ended with everyone singing "Solidarity Forever." His second long play for the Mummers involved a beautiful but "lost" heroine and several skid-row types he had researched in a St. Louis flophouse. He called it *The Fugitive Kind*, a title he would later use in connection with a different play. It received terrible notices, and a distraught Williams tried to jump out of a window. Several friends stopped him, and he himself is not sure if he would have jumped or not.

Williams' second play was a romantic drama about a young married couple living life's dream in a garret. The prize was a silver cake dish which his mother still has. He was disappointed: he expected money.

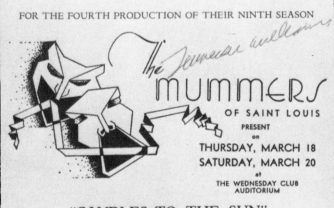

FOR THE FOURTH PRODUCTION OF THEIR NINTH SEASON

The *Tennessee Williams*

MUMMERS
OF SAINT LOUIS
PRESENT
on
THURSDAY, MARCH 18
SATURDAY, MARCH 20
at
THE WEDNESDAY CLUB
AUDITORIUM

"CANDLES TO THE SUN"
By THOMAS LANIER WILLIAMS
Directed by Willard H. Holland

CAST

BRAM PILCHER	Wesley Gore
HESTER	Genevieve Albers
STAR	Jane Garrett
JOEL (as a boy)	Donald Smith
MARY WALLACE	Jean Fischer
TIM ADAMS	Al Hohengarten
FERN	Viola Perle
LUKE (as a boy)	Lewis Turner
MRS. ABBEY	Mae Novotny
ETHEL SUNTER	Mary Hohenberger
LUKE	Sam Halley, Jr.
BIRMINGHAM RED	Willard Holland
JOEL	Gene Durnin
WHITEY SUNTER	Fred Birkicht
SEAN O'CONNOR	Frank Novotny
1st MINER	Leland Brewer
2nd MINER	Ralph Johanning
3rd MINER	George Drosten
TERRORIST LEADER	Joseph Giarraffa
MINERS' WIVES	Lucile Williamson, Ann Bono, Irene Wisdom, Lillian Byrd

Other Miners, Women and a Gang of Terrorists.

SCENE: THE PLAY TAKES PLACE IN A MINING CAMP IN THE RED HILL SECTION OF ALABAMA.

SCENE 1. BRAM PILCHER'S CABIN.
SCENE 2. THE SAME. THAT EVENING.
SCENE 3. THE SAME. FIVE YEARS LATER.
SCENE 4. STAR'S CABIN. FIVE YEARS LATER.
INTERMISSION
SCENE 5. BRAM'S CABIN. FEW MONTHS LATER.
SCENE 6. THE SAME. LATE AFTERNOON.
SCENE 7. THE SAME. EVENING.
SCENE 8. STAR'S CABIN. TWO DAYS LATER.
SCENE 9. THE SAME. IMMEDIATELY FOLLOWING.
SCENE 10. BRAM'S CABIN. SOME WEEKS LATER.

In "CANDLES TO THE SUN," the Mummers bring to their audience the third new play by a St. Louis playwright to be produced within the last year. We feel that the production of new plays is a necessary and important contribution to the growth of the non-professional theatre. Other St. Louis playwrights are urged to submit their scripts for reading.

4477 OLIVE   **THE MUMMERS OF SAINT LOUIS**   FRanklin 8416

BOARD OF DIRECTORS—Sam Halley, Jr., Genevieve Albers, Bernard Galvin, Leland Brewer, Frank Novotny, Wesley Gore, Mae Novotny, Viola Perle, Ruth Moon.
TICKETS—Aeolian Ticket Office, 1004 Olive, CHestnut 8828.
ACTIVE MEMBERSHIP—Mrs. Frank Novotny, 4477 Olive, Franklin 8416.
GENERAL PROGRAM—Rehearsals, Classes, Business Activity at Mummer Studio, 4477 Olive, FRanklin 8416.
PRODUCTION STAFF—Leland Brewer, Robert Bennett, John Allen, Miriam Schwarz, Ruth Moon, Gene Durnin.

COMING! — TWO SPRING COMEDIES

"THREE IN A ROW"	"GENTLEMEN WEAR GLOVES"
THE WILD PIECE OF NONSENSE ABOUT THE MURGATROYD TRIPLETS, SET AGAINST THE BACKGROUND OF THE ELEGANT 'EIGHTIES.	THE DROLL STORY OF A MAN WITH NEW IDEAS ABOUT STARTING A BANK PANIC.

In *The Fugitive Kind*, Mummer's director, Willard Holland (center), appeared with Samuel Halley, Jr., and Viola Perle in a tough Humphrey Bogart type role. He agreed with the adverse criticism concerning the play's sensational plot and inept construction, but he was amazed at the fantastic life Williams breathed into his characters. Even minor characters were so strongly drawn that they threatened to overshadow the leads. He found Williams easy to work with, but the Williams laugh, famous even then, threatened to drive him insane.

St. Louis Post-Dispatch

Clark Mills was the most talented poet on campus at Washington University when he became Williams' first close friend in St. Louis. A distinguished French scholar as well, he became a gentle critic of Williams' poetry, and helped expose him to a wide range of writers that included Chekhov, Lorca, Whitman, Melville, and Hart Crane.

Courtesy of Washington University, St. Louis, Missouri

Drawing by John Johns

CRANE IN MEXICO, 1931·

Above all other American poets, Williams admires Hart Crane. He sees in Crane not only his greatness but his tragedy. In this drawing made from a photograph taken by Katherine Anne Porter in Mixcoac, Mexico, less than a year before his death, Crane wears a favorite costume and the silver bridle given to him by the minister of nearby Benefinicia. After failing to start an epic poem about Mexico, Crane sailed for home aboard the SS *Orizaba*, the same ship which had brought him to Mexico. On April 26, 1932, just after noon some ten miles off the Jupiter Light out of sight of the Florida coast, Crane leaped from the stern of the ship to his death in the sea, thus achieving a transcendent unity through his favorite symbol.

Williams' early life was amazingly parallel to Hart Crane's. He has acquired a fan and a wool scarf which belonged to the poet. He has recorded favorite sections from *The Bridge* and other Crane poems. A codicil in his will calls for his body to be "sewn up in a clean white sack and dropped over board twelve hours north of Havana, so that my bones may rest not too far from those of Hart Crane."

SKETCH BY JOHN JOHNS FROM A PHOTOGRAPH BY KATHERINE ANNE PORTER

T. L. Williams Wins First in Wednesday Club Verse Contest

Miss Reka Neilson, Mary Institute Student, Awarded Junior Prize.

Thomas L. Williams, Washington University senior, 6634 Pershing avenue, was awarded the first prize of $25 in the senior division of the Wednesday Club original verse contest yesterday and Miss Reka Neilson, senior at Mary Institute, daughter of Dr. and Mrs. C. H. Neilson, 6319 Alexander drive, won the $25 first prize in the junior poetry contest. The awards were made at a meeting of the poetics section of the club, 4506 Westminster place. Mrs. Robert L. Latzer, chairman of the section, presided.

First honorable mention in the senior contest went to Miss Cevil D. Mitchell, Washington University graduate student, 4379 Westminster place, for a poem entitled "Winter." Miss Bliss McConnell, 401 North Newstead avenue, a graduate of John Burroughs School, won second honorable mention with a double quatrain, "He Has Seen Beauty."

Winners were chosen from 420 poems submitted by 123 contestants. The judges were Prof. Frank Webster of Washington University, Rev. Truman B. Douglass of the Pilgrim Congregational Church, and Rev. Louis W. Forrey, S. J. of St. Louis University, who awarded the prizes.

Won Short Story Prize.

Williams, who is 24, is the son of Mr. and rMs. Cornelius C. Williams. He was graduated from University City High School and for three years attended the University of Missouri School of Journalism. Now a senior at Washington University, he was winner last year of the Writers' Guild Short story prize. The first prize he ever won was for a poem entitled "Ode to Sara Teasdale," who was instrumental in starting the poetry competition here 11 years ago.

The opening sonnet from his prize-winning sequence, entitled "Sonnets for the Spring," follows:

Singer of Darkness.

I feel the onward rush of spring once more
Breaking upon the unresistant land
And foaming up the dark hibernal shore
As turbulent waves unfurled on turbid sand!
The cataclysm of the uncurled leaf,
The soundless thunder of the bursting green
Stuns every field. The sudden war is brief,
And instantly the flag of truce is seen,
The still, white blossom raised upon the bough!
Singer of darkness, oh, be silent now!
Raise no defense, dare to erect no wall,
But let the living fire ,the bright storm fall
With lyric paeans of victory once more
Against your own blindly surrendered shore!)"

28

THREE POETRY CONTEST WINNERS

—Staff Photo.

WINNERS of first prizes awarded yesterday in the two poetry contests sponsored by the Wednesday Club and chairman of the poetics section of the club which supervises the contest. Left to right: Thomas L. Williams, 24, Washington University senior, who won the senior contest with a sequence of three sonnets; Mrs. Robert L. Latzer, chairman of the poetics section; and Miss Reka Neilson, 16, senior at Mary Institute, who won the junior contest with "Siesta Portraits," three poems of New Mexico. The prizes were awarded yesterday at a meeting at the club, 4506 Westminster place.

Following his poetry award, Williams received a touching letter from his father's sister that said in part:

DEAREST TOM:

I scarcely know how to write to you about your beautiful sonnets . . . oh, son, I do so rejoice in this gift of yours and I know you will hold it inviolate—never cheapen it—make it count for all that is noble and fine and for that which contributes to the very best. . . . Oh, I long for you to go on and on—and son, never let anyone discourage you by attempting to measure your success by the money you make . . . this poor world has sordid ways of counting things—but take the high way, Tom, and never mind the world.

With dearest love to my dear singer—

AUNT BELLE

At Iowa, Williams made his acting debut in the University Theatre, since renamed for the late Professor E. B. Mabie, with whom Williams studied experimental playwriting.

He played a rouged, hair-teased pageboy in *Richard of Bordeaux*, and sat trembling on the forestage polishing a helmet while waiting for his one line.

He wrote a long romantic play for Mabie called *Spring Storm*, and it is the only long Williams play to ever have been lost. He also wrote a controversial radio script which ran into censorship problems. Rodney Erickson, his classmate/producer, quit the show in protest, but years later had the satisfaction of hearing echoes from this early script in *The Glass Menagerie*.

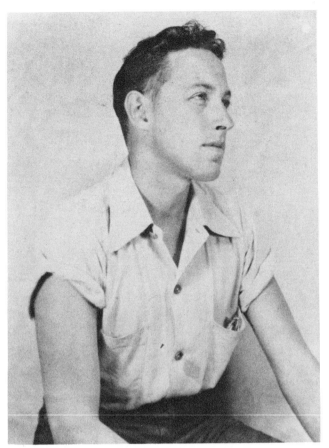

Williams had attended three colleges over a period of six years when he graduated from the University of Iowa in the summer of 1938 with a B.A. degree. He was twenty-seven years old.

PART 2

In the Winter of Cities

2

In the Winter of Cities

The cities swept about me like dead leaves,
leaves that were brightly colored but torn away
from the branches.

—Tom
The Glass Menagerie

Tennessee Williams left St. Louis in the fall of 1938, a poet/vagabond attempting, like Tom in *The Glass Menagerie*, to find in motion what was lost in space. He would never stop searching.

In Chicago he was turned down by the WPA Writers Project because he refused to say that his family was destitute. In New Orleans they told him (of all things) that his work lacked social content.

Life in the Vieux Carré overwhelmed him with its excesses. There in the old quarter, among the habitués, the lonely, the rootless, and the outcast, he found a special sense of kinship and the sort of freedom he'd always longed for. And in the profound difference between the city of daylight and the city of darkness, he found something more: a bohemian life-style that he quickly made his own. That winter, in fact and in name, he became "Tennessee" Williams.

His newly discovered sense of release found expression in several memorable one-act plays and stories, and some of his most interesting writing dates from this period. He would always think of himself as a poet, but he was fast developing a distinctive prose style. The WPA aside, his work revealed an acute social consciousness, and a growing development toward the highly symbolic writing that would become one of his most distinguishing trademarks. His evolving theme was the individual struggling for freedom against overwhelming and hopeless odds, of sailing against the small-craft warnings of life. The one-act play is a natural form for Williams; it reveals at once his strengths in creating vivid character through realistic dialogue while concealing his major weakness, plotting.

Quite by accident he read a newspaper announcement about a playwriting contest sponsored by the Group Theater, a spin-off organization from the Theater Guild in New York. He deducted from his age the three years spent in the shoe warehouse, and now an eligible twenty-four years old, he submitted his four long plays—*Candles to the Sun, The Fugitive Kind, Not About Nightingales,* and *Spring Storm*—together with three one-actors: *Moony's Kids Don't Cry, The Dark Room,* and *The Case of the Crushed Petunias,* which he collectively called *American Blues.*

The plays submitted, he paused only long enough to pack his portable typewriter, his treasured volume of Hart Crane, and his sandals. (He had long since shed his bank clerk image.) With a young clarinet player who owned a battered Chevy, he headed west through the open vistas to California. (Williams may have been a knight of the road, but he continued to send his laundry home.) When they ran out of gas and money in El Paso, "Grand" bailed them out with a $10 bill neatly stitched to a letter. They ducked buckshot from an irate landlady (Miss

Cactus Flower) who had an aversion to dead-beats and was alerted to their imminent departure when the Chevy unexpectedly backfired. They escaped and lived to siphon enough gas to reach Hawthorne, a suburb of Los Angeles where they settled down on a squab ranch owned by the clarinet player's uncle. Williams was commuting by bicycle to his regular job as a shoe clerk in Clark's Bootery within sight of the MGM studios in Culver City when he received the most encouraging news in his life. He won a special award from the Group Theater:

> To Tennessee Williams, 24 years old, of New Orleans, for *American Blues*, a group of three sketches which constitutes a full-length play.

He celebrated the prize money by quitting both jobs and heading south to tour Mexico with the clarinet player. They sampled cantina night life until the money gave out, and then pedaled back to California, sleeping in fields till they reached Laguna Beach, where they took over a nearby poultry ranch in exchange for their rent. Williams recalls these careless days as the happiest in his life. But then the poultry started dying, the clarinet player disappeared into the mountains, and Williams came as close as he ever would to starving to death.

During this temptation near the desert, he made one of the best decisions in his life. From among the many New York agents who wanted to represent him following his Group Theater success, he chose a lady named Audrey Wood.

She soon sent him an application for a Rockefeller grant and, shortly thereafter, a check for $35 from *Story Magazine* for "The Field of Blue Children." With the money, he took in the Exposition in San Francisco and had his typewriter repaired. Then he began writing a long play about memories and the loneliness of them. He called it *Battle of Angels.*

Heading east for New York and his first meeting with Audrey Wood, he stopped off in Taos, New Mexico, to visit Frieda Lawrence, the widow of his literary hero, D. H. Lawrence, and then briefly visited his mother in St. Louis. In New York, despite the kindness and warmth with which Audrey Wood received him, he found the people cold, aloof, and pretentious. He had returned to St. Louis when Audrey Wood called to tell him that he had won a Rock-

efeller grant of $1,000. For the first time in his life, he saw his mother cry.

He returned to New York, where Audrey had been instrumental in getting him a scholarship to study play-writing under Theresa Helburn and the late John Gassner at the New School for Social Research. Gassner, who was also a play reader for the Theater Guild, liked *Battle of Angels*, which Williams was still working on, and as a result of his enthusiastic support, the Theater Guild optioned the play. When school ended that spring, Williams headed for the beach at Provincetown to complete revisions of the play and to write what was intended to be the final scene of a long play about D. H. Lawrence. That summer he also wrote his one and only verse play, *The Purification.* In mood and in atmosphere, this play most clearly illustrates the influence of Garcia Lorca with its central theme of corruption, guilt, and atonement.

That fall he again visited Frieda Lawrence in Taos and then continued on to Mexico. He met Jane and Paul Bowles, both destined to become close personal friends, in Acapulco, and he was gaily touring the Costa Verde when his Theater Guild checks mysteriously stopped coming. He assumed the guild had canceled production plans, but actually he had neglected to leave a forwarding address in New York. He had just stepped off a bus in Los Angeles when he chanced to read in the New York *Times* that Miriam Hopkins would star in his play and that rehearsals were already scheduled. He rushed back immediately to New York.

Rehearsals for *Battle of Angels* were an exciting time for Williams, but he confided to a friend that because of some miscasting in the play, he had never felt more uncertain in his life. If he had a foreboding about the play, he was right. What he had conceived as the tragedy of a wandering poet who brings both salvation and destruction to a love-starved southern lady, thereby incurring his own crucifixion, opened in Boston on December 30, 1940, to boos from the audience and cries of outrage from the City Council. Williams had never heard an audience so infuriated. They stamped their feet, banged the seats as they walked out, and one man shook his fist at the cast. When a stagehand lit the smudge pots for the final holocaust, something went wrong and the audience was nearly asphyxiated. Williams compared it to the burning of Rome. The play was an unmitigated disaster, and it closed within the week.

In speaking of the failure of *Battle of Angels,* Williams says that the play was pretty far out for its day and that the mixture of superreligiousity and hysterical sexuality coexisting in a central character was a tactical error. John Gassner commented that the main difficulty was that Williams threw together too many of the elements he had dramatized separately in his best one-actors. He also thought that had Williams been able to exercise more restraint he would have made his mark in 1940 instead of having to wait five years for *The Glass Menagerie.*

Williams was crushed by the defeat in Boston, and he was nearly penniless. He was given $100 by the Theater Guild and told to go off and rewrite the play for a later production. The two years following the fiasco in Boston were, for Williams, years of continual effort and disappointment. They were a crucible in which his endurance—his very existence—was constantly tested by small menial jobs, endless money worries, despair, and depression. But through it all he kept his sense of humor, and as constantly as he traveled, he continued to write.

After spending a working vacation in Key West and somewhat cheered by an additional $500 from the Rockefellers, he returned to New York in the spring, and checked into the West Side Y, where he could swim. It would be his lifelong habit to choose living accommodations according to their swimming facilities. There he began to revise and reorganize an early play called *Beauty and the Beast* into a new, longer play, a fantasy about his years in the shoe warehouse. He called the new play *Stairs to the Roof.* He also started to collaborate on a play with his friend Donald Windham, and that summer he headed back to Provincetown. There he continued to revise *Battle of Angels* and work on *Stairs to the Roof,* which was destined to have only one professional production. The play is interesting chiefly because of phantasmagoric elements which would reappear in *Orpheus Descending, Camino Real,* and *The Red Devil Battery Sign.*

That fall he paused in New York only long enough to confer with Windham on *You Touched Me!* and to learn that the Theater Guild had canceled plans to revive *Battle of Angels.* Then he headed for New Orleans and the Vieux Carré. Often, when the revelries of the night had faded, his memories of Rose and his family quickened his sense of personal alienation.

He had been optimistic about a production of *Stairs to the Roof,* but when he returned to New York, nothing materialized, and he embarked on what would prove to be his most colorful period of employment. Following another eye operation, he wore a black patch which an abstract painter had decorated with a large white eye. He waited tables in the Beggar Bar in New York's Greenwich Village, shared billing with a transvestite, and recited light verse of his own composition until a dispute over tips with the dance-mime owner led to a wild scene that included flying soda bottles, an ambulance, and a squad car. Jobless now, he was taken in tow by a group of amiable drunks who admired his poetry and introduced to an aging actress who was awash in booze but no food. She kept going chiefly by occasional blood transfusions; Williams kept going on a hand-to-mouth existence. He ran the night elevator in the old San Jacinto Hotel and then headed south to spend the summer with friends in Macon, Georgia. The long hot summer was punctuated by his near arrest on suspicion of being a German spy and by long sessions reading aloud from the work of Anton Chekhov.

Audrey Wood had been unable to sell *Stairs to the Roof,* so that fall he headed south to Florida. He arrived in St. Augustine with $1.70 in his pocket and then drifted back to Jacksonville, where he managed to get a job running various communications machines for the Southern Branch of the U.S. Corps of Engineers. Following a mixup of transcontinental messages, his employment there was abruptly terminated. He had been working with a young man only recently released from a mental institution. They let Williams go but retained the other young man, leading Williams to conclude that they obviously preferred the certified lunatic.

Life in New York during the spring of 1943 was discouraging in spite of his usher's job at the Strand Theater at Forty-seventh and Broadway, and he had returned home to St. Louis when suddenly and ironically he went to Hollywood as part of a human package that included his friend Lem Ayers to work for MGM as a screenwriter. Deliverance of a kind was at hand.

From the beginning, Williams disliked the pretentiousness of Hollywood and the quality of material he was assigned to work on. He commuted to work aboard a secondhand motorscooter, much to the consternation of his friends back East. He wore on his head, not a crash helmet, but a narrow-brimmed Tyrolean hat adorned with a bright little feather. His view of Hollywood was as dim as the wartime blackouts through which he strolled after dinner with his friend Christopher Isherwood.

What he did like in Hollywood was the Chekhovian twilight of his private office, and it was there that he worked on an original screenplay adapted from his story *Portrait of a Girl in Glass*. He called it *The Gentleman Caller*, and when MGM turned it down and suspended him for refusing to "write something for Margaret O'Brien," he retired to the beach near Santa Monica and rewrote it as a stage play. And he retitled it *The Glass Menagerie*.

That summer he returned to Provincetown, and no sooner had he arrived than he received a citation from the National Institute of Arts and Letters:

> To Tennessee Williams, born in Mississippi in recognition of his dramatic works which reveal a poetic imagination and a gift for characterization that is rare in the contemporary theatre.

Audrey Wood appreciated the delicate story of *The Glass Menagerie*, and she kept it in her desk for two weeks before entrusting it to actor/producer/director Eddie Dowling, whose recent treatment of *Shadow and Substance* had impressed her. Dowling liked the play immediately. He thought that its commercial possibilities were nil and that it wouldn't make a dime, but he liked it enough to cancel a project in hand and arrange immediate backing. Then he set about casting the play.

Williams called his latest work a memory play. To his own remembrance of family life in St. Louis he fused the slow, remorseless destruction of the Wingfields, a mother and two children, trapped by circumstances beyond their control in a world from which there was no exit. In plot and story line, *The Glass Menagerie* was as simple and straightforward as *Battle of Angels* had been complex and involved.

Dowling's inspired casting brought out of semiretirement actress Laurette Taylor to play the mother whose life is paranoia. Considered by many America's greatest actress, she accepted the challenging role of Amanda with great enthusiasm. Dowling showed the script to critic George Jean Nathan, who suggested actress Julie Haydon for Laura, the crippled daughter whose world of little glass animals is more real to her than the "real" world. Anthony Ross was signed as the Gentleman Caller, and with Dowling himself playing the role of the poet son trapped in a warehouse job he despises, the play went into rehearsal.

For some time now, Williams had been preoccupied with what he called "the new plastic theater," and the staging of *The Glass Menagerie* reflected his expressionistic concept and embraced atmospheric touches, lighting, music, and a subtlety of direction in a free modern technique. His concept would prove so highly effective that set designers would invariably choose for his future work expressionistic sets. With his compelling use of symbols to emphasize and contrast with the meaning of the action and the dialogue, *The Glass Menagerie* contained everything that would become the trademark of a Williams play.

He made a brief visit home to St. Louis and held a rather awkward press conference, during which he recalled his dislike for the city and at which he met a young reporter from the *Star-Times* named William Inge. Then he joined the *Menagerie* company, which was rehearsing in Chicago.

In spite of the wild Irish personality clashes between Eddie Dowling and Laurette Taylor, usual and unusual problems with the sets and the costumes, plus a general foreboding of disaster stemming in large part from Laurette's not knowing her lines, everything came together miraculously on opening night, and *The Glass Menagerie* opened to generally excellent notices. Laurette Taylor gave a transcendent performance. But in spite of the good notices, it was touch and go for the first couple of weeks. Chicago critic Claudia Cassidy continued to plug the show and Aston Stevens saw it seven times. Slowly, Chicagoans started coming. By the third week the power of the press had saved the show, and soon it was playing to standing room only. *The Glass Menagerie* became a full-fledged hit.

Edwina Williams came to see her son's play,

and while she was a bit startled (and not terribly amused) to hear so many of her own lines coming from a blowsy actress in a faded dress, she survived the play and a rather tense meeting afterward when Laurette asked her, somewhat tactlessly, how she had liked herself on the stage. Later on, however, this backstage meeting with Laurette would become one of her favorite stories. Williams promptly signed over to his mother half the rights to *The Glass Menagerie*.

Word of the play's success preceded them to New York, and its triumphant opening there was a foregone conclusion. *The Glass Menagerie* would run on Broadway for nearly two years. It would be performed all over America and abroad, and Hollywood would film it. Next to *Our Town,* it would become the best-known American play. When the New York Drama Critics gathered in the Algonquin Hotel on April 10, 1945, they took just fifteen minutes to award nine of their fourteen votes to *The Glass Menagerie* and acclaim it the best play of the 1944–45 season.

In a prophetic interview with *Time* magazine, Williams announced that he had said all the nice things he had to say and that his future plays would be harsher. But at last, after years of struggle and disappointment, Tennessee Williams knew the embrace of the bitch goddess.

FRENCH QUARTER COURTYARD
OF THE TWO SISTERS
ROYAL STREET, NEW ORLEANS, LA.—150
New Orleans is a place famous for its old time
French Quarter Courtyards, which are a source
of great interest to tourists and visitors, who
come every year in large numbers to the city.

New Orleans—America's Most Interesting City

Called twice on Mrs.
Watson — she was out
both times but I
left my name and
will try again this
afternoon. The Parades
started last night — the
city is very gay now.
Love — Tom.

Rev. W. E. Dakin
1917 Snowden Ave.
Memphis, Tenn.

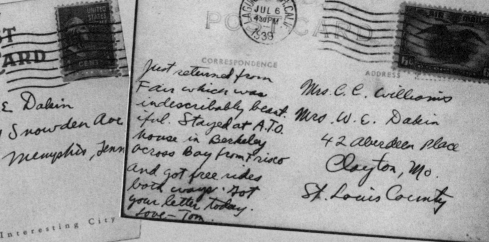

CORRESPONDENCE

Just returned from
Fair which was
indescribably beaut-
iful. Stayed at A.T.O.
house in Berkeley
across Bay from Frisco
and got free rides
both ways. Got
your letter today.
Love — Tom.

ADDRESS

Mrs. C. C. Williams
Mrs. W. E. Dakin
42 Aberdeen Place
Clayton, Mo.
St. Louis County

N-27—The Hopi Indians live upon seven
high, flat topped mesas of No. Arizona, and
are easily accessible to New Mexico travelers.
The "wise" Burro is as much a part of the
peculiar existence of this tribe of "peaceful
people" as their very strange, hand built
rock and adobe homes, perched about 500 ft
in the sky upon these formidable mesas. The
semi-arid country of Tusayan is the quaintest
and most colorful in the Southwest and these
burros are part of it.
Picture —
Me after several
adventures with
cinema and stage!
Visiting Frieda
enroute to
Clayton, for Xmas.
Address there is
33 Arundel Place.
Tennessee.

POST CARD

Audrey Wood
551 fifth Ave
New York City

The Dancing Lesson, Bobble and Alberto,
Taos, New Mexico

Dear A.W.
If you haven't already
done so, please disregard
my appeals for story
remittance as I am
leaving here at once
for St. Louis. My
address there will be
42 Aberdeen Place,
Clayton, Mo.; but God
only knows when I'll
get there as I only
have a ride as far as
Denver. Best wishes — Tennessee Williams.

Audrey Wood
Liebling Wood, Inc.
30 Rockefeller Plaza
New York City

AIR MAIL!
Via Air Mail

For Audrey —

"Whether the cup with sweet or bitter run" — Tennessee.

An early photo of Tennessee to Audrey

Above this courtyard at 722 Toulouse Street in the Vieux Carré, Williams rented an attic room for $10 a month. It would become the setting for his short story *The Angel in the Alcove*. An incident, which occurred when one of his three colorful landladies poured water down through a crack in the floor to quell a noisy group of party guests, would emerge as a pivotal situation in *Vieux Carré*.

The HISTORIC NEW ORLEANS COLLECTION

Bird imagery would one day become a well-known Williams symbol. During the summer of 1939 in California he picked squabs for his rent. He also picked up an interesting bit of philosophy: "If you hang out long enough on a corner of this coast, sooner or later a seagull is going to fly over and shit a pot of gold on you." Later that fall, when he was starving on a poultry ranch and the hens were dying by the dozens, he asked himself, "Which seagull? Which corner?" He also observed that shoveling hen shit was good practice for a young writer with Hollywood aspirations.

U.S. DEPT OF AGRICULTURE, MONTAGE BY JOHN ASHLEY

ST. LOUIS PLAYWRIGHT IS AWARDED $100 PRIZE

Thomas L. Williams, St. Louis playwright and a member of the Mummers of St. Louis, has been awarded a $100 prize for his group of one-act plays entitled, "American Blues," entered in a nation-wide playwriting contest sponsored by the Group Theater in New York, it was announced today.

Williams, son of Mr. and Mrs. Cornelius C. Williams, 42 Aberdeen place, is traveling through the west in search of material for more plays. Notification of his award came from Harold Clurman, director of the Group Theater. Among the judges of the contest was Irwin Shaw, author of "Bury the Dead." Two plays written by Williams have been produced by the Mummers. They are "Candles to the Sun" and "Fugitive Kind."

Thomas L. Williams.

Audrey Wood would represent Williams for more than thirty-two years. A partner with her husband, Bill Liebling, in their highly successful theatrical agency, Liebling/Wood, she already enjoyed a formidable reputation when she began to represent Williams. If she thought he looked "very country," she also had a very strong hunch that he was talented.

The Group Theatre Award was a big boost to his morale. He celebrated by heading South into Mexico down El Camino Real, the highway which linked the old Spanish missions like the decades on a rosary. He would pronounce the name of his play *Camino Real* to emphasize the realness of the road of life.

811 E. New Jersey
Hawthorne, Calif.

April 10, 1939

Miss Audrey Wood
Leibling-Wood
30 Rockefeller Plaza, N.Y.C.

Dear Miss Wood:

Having no acquaintance with agents I delayed answering your letter till I had communicated with Miss Thacher of the Group Theatre who has taken a very kind interest in my work. She recommends your office very highly and I am grateful for chance of such a connection. I have also been offered the services of Freida Fishbein and so it is not quite possible for me at this moment to definitely commit myself. No doubt you will also want to know more about me - so will you consult Miss Thacher or take a look at some of myscripts which may perhaps still be in her hands? Then write me again if your offer is still open - the sooner the better - and I will fully prepared by that time to make this important decision. My personal affairs are in quite a muddle justnow, I'm high and dry on the beach and may have to return back East or South within a short time - which accounts partially for my state of indecision. I would jump into the arms of any agent who could assure me the quick sale of anything - even my soul to the devil!

I want to thank you very, very much for your interest and from what Miss Thacher has written me about you I think the possibility of our association is very promising indeed.

Sincerely yours,

T. W.

TENNESSEE WILLIAMS

W. DAKIN WILLIAMS
42 ABERDEEN PLACE
CLAYTON, MISSOURI

June (?)
1939

Dear Audrey:

The girl Irene in this story from my projected novel Americans will also be, most likely, the subject of my next full-length play, making a southern trilogy, Spring Storm, Battle of Angels, and this last one which I plan to call The Aristocrats. As you have observed by now, I have only one major theme for all my work which is the destructive impact of society on the sensitive, non-conformist individual. In this case it will be an extraordinarily gifted young woman artist who is forced into prostitution and finally the end described in the story. In "B. of A." it was a boy who hungered for something beyond reality and got death by torture at the hands of a mob - I hope that idea got across in the script. Your protracted silence has begun to disturb me, my dear!

When you have read the story (with play in mind) please pass it on to Burnett as a sample of material to be used in novel which I have discussed with him.

I am still here in St. Louis by virtue of necessity - the smother of invention! All optimism has departed - I suspect and expect the worst!

I hope you are not the same,

Sincerely,

T. W.

Tenn. Wms.

Williams wrote this letter to Audrey Wood just before he headed East for New York City to meet her for the first time.

Williams banked his Rockefeller money, and Audrey Wood assumed the role of his personal banker. She doled it out to him at the rate of $25 a week, an amount supplemented by option money of $50 a month from Hume Cronyn, who was vainly trying to raise $11,000 for a Broadway production of Williams one-acters.

Williams works every morning wherever he is. In those early years it is interesting to note that his favorite haunts became such end-of-land places as New Orleans, Key West and Provincetown on Cape Cod. He attributes his drive and energy to his paternal heritage.

Williams celebrated his Theatre Guild option for *Battle of Angels* in the Village Barn on May 8, 1940, with close friends and fellow southerners Fred Melton and Donald Windham, and a sculptress named Anne Bretzfelder.

COLLECTION OF TENNESSEE WILLIAMS

Tallulah Bankhead was appearing in nearby Dennis Port during Williams' first summer in Provincetown, and he hoped she would play Myra in *Battle of Angels.* He pedaled down and left a script which she promised to read, then later returned to meet her backstage. "Oh, it's you. The play's impossible, darling, but sit down and have a drink with me." Years later, when she was touring as Regina in her greatest triumph, *The Little Foxes,* he met her back stage again. "Well, darling," she roared, "I was luckier than Miriam Hopkins, who lost her mind and actually appeared in that abominable Battle-something-or-other that you had the impertinence to write for me."

Publicity portrait for *Battle of Angels* by Vandam.

Battle of Angels

by Tennessee Williams

Pharos: Numbers 1 & 2

Spring, 1945 - $1.50

Published edition, *Battle of Angels*

Actress Miriam Hopkins had come as close as anyone to playing Scarlett O'Hara in *Gone with the Wind,* and she chose *Battle of Angels* as her comeback vehicle to the stage.

Miriam Hopkins Opens in Theater Guild's New Dram

THE THEATER

By ALEXANDER WILLIAMS

"Battle of Angels"

WILBUR

"Battle of Angeles," a drama by Tennessee Williams, directed by Margaret Webster, setting by Cleon Throckmorton, produced by Theresa Helburn and Lawrence Langner, presented by the Theater Guild, Inc., for the first time anywhere last night in the Wilbur Theater, with the following cast:

Dolly Bland	Dorothy Peterson
Beulah Cartwright	Edith King
Pee Wee Bland	Robert Einhardt
Sheriff Talbott	Charles McClelland
Cassandra Whiteside	Doris Dudley
Vee Talbot	Katherina Raht
Valentine Xavier	Wesley Addy
Eva Temple	Hazel Hanna
Blanch Temple	Helen Carewe
Myra Torrance	Miriam Hopkins
Joe	Clarence Washington
Small Boy	Bertram Holmes
Bennie	Ivan Lewis
Jabe Torrance	Marshall Bradford

Mr. Tennessee Williams has certainly written an astonishing play, one of the strangest mixtures of poetry, realism, melodrama, comedy, whimsy and eroticism that it has ever been our privilege to see upon the boards. In a sense there is something for every taste and equally something that will irritate any customer, who more or less knows his mind about theatrical matter.

For example, we happen to like Mr. Williams' sure sense of atmosphere in the Mississippi Delta town and his sense of humor in touching up the various characters who come in and out of the Torrances' store. It must also be said that Margaret Webster's direction and the Theater Guild's production have combined to make this atmosphere thoroughly effective.

But we do not happen to care for Mr. Williams' frequent dips into allegory, his occasional touches of

archness in the love-making and, above all, his mysterious hero, one of those literary wanderers who come from nowhere and depart nowhither to the utter confusion of all the other characters. Mr. Williams' hero is Val Xavier, whose "eyes shine like a dog's in the dark," and who is obsessed by the fear of five.

He tells his story to the heroine, Myra, the shopkeeper's wife. He has ever been a lonely one of the earth and lived and known love in the bayous of Tennessee. He is also writing a great book. Myra's husband is upstairs with an incurable disease and he stamps ominously on the floor at dramatic moments —downstairs—for assistance. It later appears that he is the personification of death, and very well he succeeds in his mission on earth.

Meanwhile Myra and Val are knowing a brief interlude of happiness; and Myra, who has always feared the idea of barrenness, is going to have a child by Val. But he gossips of the town and the bad woman, Cassandra Whiteside—you catch her place in the allegory?—have also fallen for Val's charms. Now he wants to escape to the desert, especially as the river is in flood, to a place where his thoughts, in the happy phrase of the author, can stretch.

The husband, Death or Jabe Torrance as you prefer, now enters the picture other than by stamping from above. A highly melodramatic scene is whipped up. Myra is shot, and an angry crowd assembles to burn up the house with Val in it. Just then Cassandra appears, having slept off her drunken jag, and tells Val that self-immolation is to be

their glorious doom. He staggers up the stairs, now alight with the glow of fire, the dead Myra in his arms. Moussorgsky had somewhat the same idea in his opera, "Khovanstchina"; and he, like Mr. Williams, rang down his curtain on this undeniably stirring scene.

As we have said, the direction and acting of this seemed to us nearly perfect. Miss Doris Dudley is absolutely splendid as the bad woman. Miriam Hopkins in the much harder role of Myra does a most convincing piece of work. Wesley Addy is not less sympathetic and appealing as the hero. All the townsfolk, the Misses Peterson, King, Raht, Carewe and Hanna, and the Messrs. Embardt and McClelland, contributed with the greatest of naturalness the most solidly satisfying moments of the play. The scene where the religious fanatic discovers that she has painted Val as Christ is uncomfortable, but that is due to our own scruples and the playwright's uncompromising realism at this point. We have never been in a mercantile store in the Mississippi Delta, but Mr. Throckmorton's set seemed just the thing.

Music and The Dance

WESTERN UNION

1201

MZD10 15/18 NT=MIAMI FLO 20   1941 MAR 20 PM 9 11

AUDREY WOOD=

    LIEBLING WOOD INC 551 FIFTH AVE NYK=

STRANDED - EVICTED HOTEL. BALKAN SITUATION COMPARATIVELY

NOTHING. IF ANTHOLOGY CHECK UNMAILED PLEASE WIRE TWENTY

DOLLARS WESTERNUNION IMMEDIATELY LOVE=

    TENNESSEE WILLIAMS.

A crestfallen Williams spent half of the $100 given him at the closing of *Battle of Angels* for the first of four operations to correct a cataract on his left eye, and was en route to Key West when the money gave out.

ST. LOUIS STAR-TIMES

Miriam Hopkins Irked When St. Louisan's Play Is Cut

BOSTON, Jan. 7.—(U. P.)—Miriam Hopkins bowed to the objections of city councilmen to certain lines in the play "Battle of Angels," but said today that the protesting city fathers ought to be "thrown into Boston harbor, as the tea once was."

"I'll bet they haven't even seen the play," the actress said. "Their attitude is an insult to the fine young man (Thomas Lanier "Tennessee" Williams of St. Louis) who wrote the show, and you can tell them for me that I haven't gotten to the point where I have to appear in dirty plays."

"Battle of Angels" is about life in the Mississippi delta region and deals at length with such things as infidelity and the consequences thereof.

City Councillor Michael J. Ward, who said he hadn't seen the play but had heard plenty about it, called it "putrid."

"It's not a dirty play," Miss Hopkins said. "If it were I wouldn't be in it. The dirt is something in the minds of some of the people who have seen it."

Police Commissioner Joseph F. Timilty and Assistant City Censor Joseph Mikolajewski ruled the show could go on if certain lines were deleted. A spokesman for the producer, the Theater Guild, said the changes would be made, but that, in any event, the play would close Saturday unless a collaborator could be found to help the author rewrite it.

Timilty described the show as "a play about cheap white trash," and much of the dialog is "improper and indecent."

The assistant censor said: "Too

MIRIAM HOPKINS.

many of the lines have double meanings."

How Williams Described Play.

Thomas Lanier Williams, St. Louis playwright who uses the name Tennessee Williams, is the son of Mr. and Mrs. Cornelius C. Williams of 42 Aberdeen place. In a recent letter from New York, he described his play, "Battle of Angels," as "a sex play with cosmic overtones."

After studying at Washington University, he worked with the University of Iowa dramatic group. The Mummers, St. Louis amateur theatrical group, has produced two of his plays. "Candles to the Sun," in March, 1937, and "Fugitive Kind," in December, 1937.

A year ago Williams won one of five $1,000 fellowships of the Rockefeller Foundation through the Rockeatists' Guild of the Authors' League of America.

22   LOTHAR WOLFF   NEW YORK

Tennessee Williams   *where I hang my hat!*

Mr & Mrs. Jesse Stuart   *Riverton, Ky.* pd

Williams was a true knight of the road when he signed "The Trade Winds'" guest register.

COURTESY OF GEORGE ROBISON BLACK

THE TRADE WINDS   **KEY WEST, FLORIDA**

Picture Postcard of "The Trade Wind" in Key West

"The Trade Winds" in Key West was a handsome landmark mansion recently opened as an inn, and managed by Clara Atwood Black, the widow of an eminent Episcopal minister. When it developed that her late husband, the Reverend Robert M. W. Black, had attended the same theological seminary at the University of the South as had Williams' grandfather Dakin, she rented him a cottage which may have been formerly a child's playhouse (shades of Ibsen) just behind the Inn for $8 a week.

COURTESY OF GEORGE ROBISON BLACK

Regis and Marion Black Vaccaro, who had recently purchased the Caroline Lowe House and named it "The Trade Winds," shared with Williams a New Orleans background. He would use their name in *27 Wagons Full of Cotton,* and again in *Baby Doll.* Of both Marion and her mother Clara Black he would one day write: "They had an heroic quality and a generosity of spirit that I found humbling to someone like myself whose introverted and nervously shattered existence walled him in from all but those few who bothered to break through the walls."

COURTESY OF GEORGE ROBISON BLACK

Dear Audrey: Please mail me Theatre Guild checque
#3 <u>toute de suite</u> if you haven't already. Have you
received any payment from Mayorga? I see her book
has come out. My play revision is about complete
in first draft and I will send you synopsis of what
I've done. If I don't finish a satisfactory job
before the funds are exhausted I suppose I will
have to join some branch of military service. Will
consider anything in Hollywood that Liebling knows
of. - Meeting loads of famous people such as
Grant Wood, Max Eastman, Benedict Thielen, John
Dewey, Arnold Branch, Doris Lee - Arthur Arent
who was here thinks Warners might like "Angels"
for Bette Davis.. Lovely idea anyway.

Off to the beach. Love.

10 % "Trade winds"
Key West.
Fla.

Williams returned to New York City that fall, checked into the West Side
"Y," and immediately began to reorganize an early play (*Beauty and the
Beast*) into a fantasy about his life in the shoe warehouse, thus beginning
his life-long habit of revising earlier work into newer, longer forms. He
retitled the play *Stairs to the Roof.*

COLLECTION OF TENNESSEE WILLIAMS

49

Anton Chekhov is the single most important influence on Williams' work. Echoes of Chekhov's approach to organic writing are evident in Williams' emphasis on characterization. Like Chekhov, Williams invests ordinary events with spiritual significance. Both writers share the same sense of the isolation of human beings and their tragic inability to communicate with each other. As Chekhov's milieu was the dying aristocracy of feudal Russia, so Williams celebrates the antebellum South. Like Chekhov, Williams poses the great questions but leaves them unanswered. His judge in *The Purification* says, "I do not believe in one man judging another; I'd rather that those who stand in need of judgment would judge themselves."

ANTON TCHEKHOV IN 1883

D. H. Lawrence was a highly simpatico figure in Williams' literary upbringing. He was interested in Lawrence's symbols, his cosmic views of sex, his love/hatred of women, his fierce hunger for life, and his anguished search for God. Williams would later write, "Lawrence felt the mystery and power of sex as the primal life urge and was the life-long adversary of those who wanted to keep the subject locked away in the cellar of prudity. Much of his work is chaotic and distorted by tangent obsessions, such as his insistence upon the woman's subservience to the male, but all in all, his work is probably the greatest modern monument to the dark roots of creation."

50

Williams, who had twice been medically rejected for military service, briefly worked in communications on the graveyard shift for the Southern Branch of the U.S. Army Engineers in Jacksonville, Florida. During the early morning hours he had time to think about which parts of *Don Quixote* might lend themselves to a dramatic statement about the disaster of all ideals and knight errantry, and the death of the chivalric principle. In years to come, *Camino Real* would emerge as the most exciting new play Broadway had seen in years.

Williams capped his two years in limbo by neatly fitting the uniform or an usher friend at the Strand Theatre on Broadway and 47th Street, and in 1943, any uniform was a blessing. He recalls the blue and gold uniform as one of the handsomest outfits he's ever worn. He stood in a small pool of light, and with an elaborate gesture of his white-gloved hands directed patrons to the exits. He always managed to catch Dooley Wilson sing "As Time Goes By" during the long run of *Casablanca.* He would dedicate *The Last of My Solid Gold Watches* to Sidney Greenstreet.

In spite of his usher's salary of $17 a week, the struggle to survive in New York ended when he returned to St. Louis. His first assignment was to have been *The Sun Is My Undoing,* but instead he was put to work on *Marriage Is a Private Affair,* starring Lana Turner. Williams worked hard and well for the picture, but producer Pandro Berman told him his dialogue was beyond Miss Turner's talent. Williams could only remember the film as *"The Celluloid Brassiere."*

THEATRE AND DANCE COLLECTION MUSEUM OF THE CITY OF NEW YORK

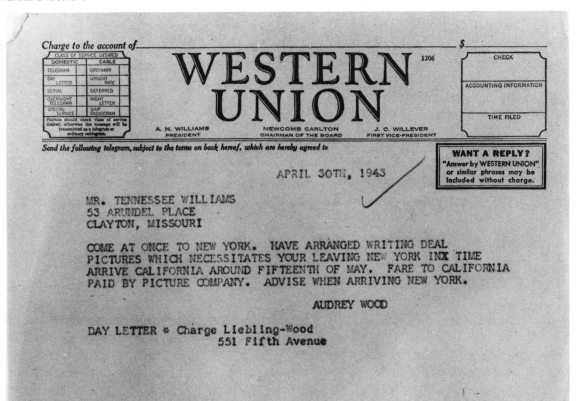

Dear Audrey:

Here is the story I promised you some time ago. Originally
it was thirty-two pages and a bloody mess. I think the present
version may have an effective simplicity. It is a minor excursion
into the same material I am using for the stage version of "The
Gentleman Caller". I am sure you will think the material too
slight toø sustain a long play, but the play will embody a good
deal more than the story would suggest.

Here is a scenic out-line of the play-script, which the story may
help you to follow.

> I.   Christmas Eve. Amanda's presents to her children
> are a fiasco. She gives Tom two books on how to be
> an executive and the secret of salesmanship. To Laura
> she gives a six-months course at Rubicam's business
> college.
>
> II.   Laura's bedroom, the sanctuary of glass, is revealed
> by lifting the back wall of the permanent set (living-room).
> Scene between Laura, in bed with influenza, and Mother
> just returned from business-college where she has made
> the appalling discovery of Laura's truancy in park and
> pretense.
>
> (Amanda has been working as a model for matron's dresses
> at down-town dept. store and has just lost the job be-
> cause of faded appearance.)
>
> Amanda decides the only remaining course open for Laura
> is marraige.
>
> III.   A Sunday dinner. A long monolgue by Amanda recalling
> the Sunday afternoons in Blue Mountain when she entertained
> as many as seventeen gentleman callers. It is high time,
> by implication, that Laura entertained at least one.
>
> IV.   Amanda, at breakfast, exhorts Tom to produce a
> gentleman caller for Laura. Must be one at the warehouse.

Once there is a man to take his place in the family, he will be free, she assures him, to crawl out from under his present responsibilities to the household.

V. Spurred by this promise, Tom has invited a shipping-clerk to dinner for the following Friday. He gives Amanda this electrifying news and she begins to make suitable plans for the occasion.

VI. Amanda on the phone, conducting an impassioned campaign to sell subscription to "The Housekeeper's Companion". Object to finance new clothes for Laura to receive her caller.

VII. The Night of the Gentleman Caller." Amanda has given the occasion an atmosphere of terrifying importance and Laura is thrown into a nervous panic.

Scene preceding dinner. - Dinner Scene. - Scene after dinner.

Love touches Laura and is swept away with the disclosure the young man is already committed to another girl.

Amanda "lights into" Tom and there is a furious verbal battle, oblivious to Laura's hurt.

VIII. Late at night, following Tom's losing job at warehouse.

He says goodbye to the apartment, but leaves without to Mother or Laura.

IX. The Morning. Tom's flight discovered. Amanda breaks down and everything seems to have fallen into an irreparable ruin.

For once Laura is the pillar of strength. She quietly accepts the disaster and understands and forgives the dereliction of Tom.

But defeat is not for Amanda, no more than momentarily. Let the two men, Tom and his father, pursue whatever they want from their faithless and selfish vagrancy. They, the two women, can build a world without them.

Following his suspension for refusing to write something for teary Margaret O'Brien ("Child stars make me vomit"), Williams retired to a pleasant apartment near the Santa Monica beach. He wrote a story about his landlady called "The Mattress by the Tomato Patch," and he offered MGM an original screenplay called *The Gentleman Caller*. Producer William Fadiman turned it down, and Williams rewrote it as a stage play, eventually renaming it *The Glass Menagerie*.

Margo Jones, "The Texas Tornado," was an early and ardent Williams admirer. She founded the Dallas theater-in-the-round and worked as assistant director to Eddie Dowling on *The Glass Menagerie*. She would later produce and direct *Summer and Smoke*. She became a warm personal friend, and her tragic death in 1955 cost the theater one of its most dynamic personalities.

COLLECTION OF TENNESSEE WILLIAMS

CHICAGO STAGEBILL

Laurette Taylor was a legend in the theater before Tennessee Williams was born. Her greatest success had been in her husband, Hartley Manner's play, *Peg of My Heart.* For some time since his death, she had gradually dropped out of sight, submerged in alcohol. When Dowling offered her the mother's role in *Menagerie,* she immediately saw the challenge of the characterization (her strongest talent), and she accepted joyously. Her performance would be called one of the greatest comebacks in the history of the American theater. Sadly, it was her last role.

Williams had wanted Donald Windham to write the screen adaption of *The Glass Menagerie,* but it was not to be. Lovely Gertrude Lawrence was hopelessly miscast, and when Hollywood wanted to put Tom aboard a ship, Williams observed that he hoped they wouldn't put Amanda on skates. In spite of Kirk Douglas, Arthur Kennedy, and Jane Wyman, somewhere between the stage and the screen, all the poetry was lost. Williams considers *The Glass Menagerie* the worst film ever made of his work.

Williams took a nap before the Washington Command Performance and never did wake up in time to attend the White House reception. Company members were hard put to explain his absence to President Truman.

15 DEC. 1946.
N.Y. TIMES

SCREEN

AN APPRECIATION

Creator of 'The Glass Menagerie' Pays Tribute to Laurette Taylor

By TENNESSEE WILLIAMS

NEW ORLEANS.

I DO not altogether trust the emotionalism that is commonly indulged in over the death of an artist, not because it is necessarily lacking in sincerity but because it may come too easily. In what I say now about Laurette Taylor I restrict myself to those things which I have felt continually about her as apart from any which this unhappy occasion produces.

Of course the first is that I consider her the greatest artist of her profession that I have known. The second is that I loved her as a person. In a way the second is more remarkable. I have seldom encountered any argument about her pre-eminent stature as an actress. But for me to love her was remarkable because I have always been so awkward and diffident around actors that it has made a barrier between us almost all but insuperable.

In the case of Laurette Taylor, I cannot say that I ever got over the awkwardness and the awe which originally were present, but she would not allow it to stand between us. The great warmth of her heart burned through and we became close friends.

I am afraid it is the only close friendship I have ever had with a player.

Gallant Performer

Gallantry is the word that best fits those human qualities which made Laurette Taylor so intensely lovable as a person. I do not think it is realized how much she sacrificed of her personal comfort and health during the year and a half that she played in "The Glass Menagerie." She remained in the part that long because of a heroic perseverance I find as magnificent as her art itself. It is not necessary to mention the mistaken reservation some people had about her ability to remain long with a play.

But Laurette was painfully aware of that reservation and was determined to beat it. She did. She was neither a well nor strong person at any time during the run of the play and often continued her performance when a person of ordinary spirit would not have dared to. Even when throat trouble made it painful for her to speak she continued in her demanding part and I have never seen her physical suffering affect the unfailing wonder of her performance.

It is our immeasurable loss that Laurette Taylor's performances were not preserved on the modern screen. The same is true of Duse and Bernhardt, with whom her name belongs. Their glory survives in the testimony and inspiration of those who saw them. Too many people have been too deeply moved by the gift of Laurette Taylor for that to disappear from us.

In this unfathomable experience of ours there are sometimes hints of something that lies outside the flesh and its mortality. I suppose these intuitions come to many people in their religious vocations, but I have sensed them more clearly in the work of artists and most clearly of all in the art of Laurette Taylor. There was a radiance about her art which I can compare only to the greatest lines of poetry, and which gave me the same shock of revelation as if the air about us had been momentarily broken through by light from some clear space beyond us.

Playwright's Reward

The last word that I received from her was a telegram which reached me early this fall. It was immediately after the road com-

Laurette Taylor.

pany of our play had opened in Pittsburgh. The notices spoke warmly of Pauline Lord's performance in the part of Amanda. "I have just read the Pittsburgh notices," Laurette wired me. "What did I tell you, my boy? You don't need me."

I feel now—as I have always felt—that a whole career of writing for the theatre is rewarded enough by having created one good part for a great actress. Having created a part for Laurette Taylor is a reward I find sufficient for all the effort that went before and any that may come after.

REMEMBER THE NEEDIEST!

57

Beginning with *The Glass Menagerie*, Williams would eventually be published in 48 languages. His plays would be produced throughout the world, and *The Glass Menagerie* would become his most often performed work.

With *The Glass Menagerie* came success—that always longed for, always expected something that Williams lived for. But already he was suffering from the catastrophe of it.

The Winner

For the first time in its ten-year history, the New York Drama Critics' Circle last week chose the season's best American play on the first ballot. The choice, Tennessee Williams' touching picture of a troubled family, *The Glass Menagerie* (TIME, April 9), easily met the majority requirement with nine out of 14 votes.*

The Glass Menagerie is 31-year-old Playwright Williams' first Broadway production. But he has written eight other plays; including *Battle of Angels*, which the Theater Guild closed out of town four years ago, and *You Touched Me*, which Guthrie McClintic plans to bring

Ann Rosener-Pix
TENNESSEE WILLIAMS
No more nice things?

to Broadway this fall. Though delighted by the award, Williams demurred: "I think *The Deep Mrs. Sykes* should have gotten the prize." He also doubted whether "the critics will like my future plays as much as this one. In this play I said all the nice things I have to say about people. The future things will be harsher."

Mississippi-born Playwright Williams has done many things besides write plays. Since graduating from the State University of Iowa, he has been a bellhop, an elevator operator, a movie usher, a teletyper, a warehouse handyman, a waiter and spouter of verse in a Greenwich Village nightclub. He has also changed his name, because he thought his real name, Thomas Lanier Williams, "sounded too much like William Lyon Phelps."

* Other votes: two for *Harvey;* one each for *A Bell for Adano* and *I Remember Mama.* One critic voted that no award be made.

PART 3

Dramatist of Lost Souls

3

Dramatist of Lost Souls

In the middle of the journey of our life, I came
to myself in a dark wood where the straight way
was lost.

—Dante's *Inferno*
Canto I

The success of *The Glass Menagerie* snatched Williams out of virtual oblivion and thrust him into instant celebrity status. He was lionized, patronized—and victimized—to the point where he welcomed the gauze mask which covered his eyes following the fourth and last operation on his left eye. With the world shut out of sight, he saw things in their true perspective.

When he left the hospital, he headed for Mexico, stopping in Dallas to visit Margo Jones, who was rehearsing an early version of *Summer and Smoke* for her theater-in-the-round.

The high altitude of Mexico was invigorating; he wrote the celebrated story "One Arm" and worked on a play he had started in Chicago during rehearsals for *Menagerie*, a play he thought of as a tragedy of incomprehension. It had evolved through three titles: *Blanche's Chair in the Moon, The Moth,* and *The Primary Colors.* Its current title was *The Poker Night*; it would become *A Streetcar Named Desire.* Williams first visualized Blanche sitting alone in a chair with the moonlight streaming through the window on her, waiting for a beau who didn't show up. He had completed about fifty pages of the script but put it aside to work on *Summer and Smoke,* a play he had originally called *A Chart of Anatomy.*

That fall he returned to New York for rehearsals and the Broadway opening of *You Touched Me!*, his collaboration with Donald Windham

about a virile young man who invades a group of spinsters and causes the commotion of a fox in the chicken coop. When the play opened, it suffered immediately from a critical comparison to *The Glass Menagerie* which had been written later than *You Touched Me!* but produced earlier. Mixed notices closed the new play in a few months, and it is one of the few Williams plays not to be rewritten or reprinted.

Shortly after Christmas that year he took his first apartment in New Orleans, near the St. Louis Cathedral. There he wrote a strange little play called *10 Blocks on the Camino Real* but put it away at his agent's suggestion, something he later regretted, thinking that had he reworked it then he might have made something beautiful out of it instead of the flawed piece it later became. He also wrote a one-act play called *The Long Stay Cut Short,* or *The Unsatisfactory Supper,* which introduced Aunt Rose Comfort as the aged dependent relative who cooks supper but forgets to light the stove first.

That summer he fled the heat of New Orleans and with a companion was driving to visit Frieda Lawrence in New Mexico when his secondhand car collapsed. He himself was experiencing severe abdominal pains, and shortly after the car expired, he was hospitalized in a small Catholic hospital near Taos. Despairing of his life, he made his will and then underwent a four-hour operation, thinking just before he went under that the nuns, sinister-looking in their black habits, were elderly usherettes in the great lobby of the beyond.

He left the hospital much too soon, and he was careering up a mountain with Frieda at the wheel when he experienced difficult breathing. He was rushed back to the hospital, and when he was discharged, he refused to invest in a new suit, thinking he wouldn't live long enough to recoup the investment.

That summer he journeyed to Nantucket Island, the ancestral home of his Coffin relatives, and rented a modest beach house for the few months he thought he'd live. He had greatly admired Carson McCullers' novel *The Member of the Wedding*, and he very much wanted to meet her. At the suggestion of her cousin Jordan Massee, he wrote her a fan letter and invited her to visit him. They worked that summer at either end of a table, he on *Summer and Smoke*, and she on a dramatization of her novel. They became close, lifelong friends.

In New Orleans that fall Williams took a lovely second-floor apartment in the Vieux Carré. And it was there that he retitled *The Poker Night*; to *A Streetcar Named Desire*.

Toward spring, to his intense pleasure, his Grandfather Dakin came to live with him. The old gentleman's presence was a tonic to Williams; they summered in Key West atop La Concha Hotel, and spurred on by his happiness, Williams completely rewrote *Streetcar* in one month flat. Later that summer he journeyed to Charleston, South Carolina, met producer Irene Selznick, and that same evening, signed the contracts for the new play.

Williams had very much admired the direction of Arthur Miller's play *All My Sons*, and he implored Selznick to sign its director, Elia Kazan, for *Streetcar*. Through the efforts of Molly Thatcher, now Kazan's wife and the same person who had recommended Williams and Audrey Wood to each other back during his Group Theater success, Kazan agreed to direct the play.

In the weeks ahead Williams would travel to the West Coast and meet a lovely young actress named Jessica Tandy. He would also interview a young man from the Actors' Studio, and in Provincetown that summer he would meet Frank Phillip Merlo.

Streetcar went into rehearsal in New York, but despite the enthusiasm surrounding the script, Williams despaired of the play's success. He also imagined he had pancreatic cancer.

They were on the road in Boston when the play started to get good notices, and in Philadelphia, Kazan finally turned to him and said, "This smells like a hit." And so it was. *Streetcar* opened in New York to unanimous rave notices.

The tremendous success of *Streetcar* was doubly sweet for Williams. He had been annoyed at having been dismissed by some critics as a one-shot playwright who had written the autobiographical play *The Glass Menagerie*, and the huge success of the new play did much to assuage his wounded pride. It was an extremely satisfying time in his life.

In midsummer Williams left the old brownstone in Manhattan's Chelsea district, took some of his $2,000-a-week royalties, and sailed aboard the *America* for Europe. In Paris he visited Carson McCullers and her husband, Reeves, observed Cocteau's aberrant production of *Streetcar*, and deliberately avoided both the Brighton and London openings of *The Glass Menagerie*. He also met a young American writer named Gore Vidal, with whom he shared many merry times during what they would come to call "the golden age." Theirs would be a friendship with many hiatuses, few quarrels.

In Italy Williams began a lifelong love affair with that country and its people. He interrupted his European vacation that fall to catch the London production of *The Glass Menagerie* with Helen Hayes, then, with Truman Capote for company, sailed home aboard the *Queen Mary* for the New York opening of *Summer and Smoke*.

As was the case with *You Touched Me!* and *The Glass Menagerie*, *Summer and Smoke* had been written earlier than *Streetcar* but produced later while *Streetcar* was still doing big business, and of course, *Summer and Smoke* suffered from the inevitable comparison. Williams felt that to bring such an atmospheric play to New York and present it in a large theater would be a calculated risk that might destroy its charm and send its buoyant liveliness disappearing into the fly loft, and he was right. The play was disappointingly received, and Williams was crushed. With companions Frank Merlo and Paul Bowles, he sailed aboard the *Vulcania* for North Africa.

They toured wildly before passing through Gibraltar to Italy, where Williams' natural good humor was quickly restored. He found in the Italian people much of the excitement, the naturalness, and the grace he had found in the people of Mexico. He was still depressed by the critical failure of *Summer and Smoke*, but as his spirits revived, he began to expand a short story called "Moon of Pause" into a first novel. It was also his first Italian work; he called it *The Roman Spring of Mrs. Stone.*

In this chronicle of life after death, he transferred to Karen Stone, a wealthy retired actress, lonely and depressed following the recent death of her husband, much of the same sense of "drift" that he himself felt following the New York closing of *Summer and Smoke.* The novel traces the gradual decline of an aging woman sinking inexorably into destruction and degeneration in a struggle against time, against the decay of female virtue and the decadence of age. Williams contrasted the barren American materialistic outlook with the vital sexuality of the Italian in the lush Roman springtime and invoked time as an antagonist, something he would repeat in *Sweet Bird of Youth.*

Later that year Frank Merlo introduced him to Sicily, and everything in that country's culture appealed to him. He loved it even more than the Italian mainland. He worked on *Camino Real,* his play about Don Quixote and the destruction of the romantic spirit, but he also began a second Italian work, a long play which reflected the warmth and sweetness of the Sicily he was growing to love. In this comedy with strong tragic overtones, he combined the South he knew with the warmth and expressionism of the Mediterranean. After two title changes, it became *The Rose Tattoo.*

Williams saw Serafina della Rosa, her little house, her little proprieties, as a delicate, tissue-paper fence built lovingly around the instinct to protect and preserve that which is the meaning of Woman, as opposed to the bleating of the goats, the cries of the children, the wind banging the shutters, the roar of the trucks on the highway as the fierce omnipresent element of chance and destruction, as the careless universe that besieges this little woman-built cosmos or womb.

The play glorifies sexuality and celebrates, more than any other Williams play, the mystical symbolism of the rose. Although the play was criticized for an overabundance of symbolism, critics also viewed it as a departure from, rather than as a development toward, his natural dramatic writing.

Originally he had wanted Italy's greatest actress, Anna Magnani, for the New York production, but her English simply wasn't up to the New York stage. Still, she did agree to make the film. Originally it was her idea to shoot the film in Sicily with Marlon Brando, who would play an American GI of Sicilian descent stationed there during the postwar occupation. But *The Rose Tattoo* would be filmed in Key West, Florida, and she would co-star with Burt Lancaster.

Since the day Williams had stopped in at the Actors' Studio in New York and caught part of a Kazan rehearsal for his short play *10 Blocks on the Camino Real,* and exclaimed, "Oh, Gadge, we must do this," he had worked on the play and expanded it to full length. Kazan cast the show entirely from the Actors' Studio, and *Camino Real* opened as the second collaboration between Broadway's two hottest talents. It created the most excitement the New York theater had seen in years.

The play, an affirmative statement about the ultimate victory of the romantic spirit, unfolds in sixteen blocks, or scenes. Into the Camino Real—a dead-end plaza from which there is no escape—wanders Don Quixote, the personification of all the world's romantics. He lies down to sleep and to dream a pageant, a masque of humanity from whose parade of literary figures, riffraff, spoiled romantics, and romantic spoilers he will choose a successor to his squire Sancho, who has deserted him.

Into this nightmare world, this bazaar where the human heart is part of the bargain, wanders Kilroy, the legendary American hero, a bewildered innocent, looking only for a fair chance and a place to rest in a world which offers him only degradation and humiliation. He finds neither, but he has a redeeming idealism and believes that just being alive is purpose enough for living.

Every playgoer became a critic! Some found it murky and chaotic; others called it clear and relentlessly honest. The New York critics found the former and the play became Williams' most personal critical failure. As was the case with *Summer and Smoke,* it would take Jose Quintero's Circle in the Square production to vindicate a play into which Williams had put so much of himself. In the meantime, it was a bitter personal defeat.

Years earlier, Williams had written a charming mood piece called *Three Players of a Summer Game.* From this novella he developed a long play about family relationships called *Cat on a Hot Tin Roof.* He envisioned the play in three separate acts or scenes: the first between husband and wife, the second between father and son, and the third a family conference. The play is unique in that there is no time lapse. The action of the play takes place in the exact time that the play occupies the theater.

Elia Kazan liked the new play very much, but he had a few reservations about the third act. Mainly, he felt that Big Daddy was too important a character to appear only in the second act. Williams has since said that he violated his own intuition by bringing Big Daddy back onstage in the third act, but he very much wanted Kazan to direct the play, and so he had Big Daddy return and tell the famous "elephant story" which had to be eliminated because of the New York censors. Williams prefers his original ending.

Cat on a Hot Tin Roof was hailed by critics as the work of a mature artist. Williams himself says that it comes closest to being a work of art and a work of craft than anything else he has ever written. His name and reputation had been made by *The Glass Menagerie* and *A Streetcar Named Desire,* and *Cat* became his most financially rewarding play, although he would later dream in France that *Cat* was a failure and wake up thinking he was broke.

Tallulah Bankhead appeared in a Miami revival of *Streetcar* in the mid 1950s, and Williams became a frequent visitor to the Coconut Grove area. Marion Vaccaro had recently moved into her new home on Biscayne Bay, and aside from the Coconut Grove Playhouse, which he considered one of the most beautiful Off-Broadway houses in the nation, the relaxed atmosphere and the nearby facilities of George Keathley's Studio "M" playhouse were just right for an early tryout of a work in progress. The new play was about lost youth and the betrayal of people's hearts by the subtle progress of corruption both spiritual and material. He called it *Sweet Bird of Youth.*

Shortly after Bankhead's appearance at the Grove Playhouse, *Sweet Bird* went into rehearsal at Studio "M" with George Keathley directing. For everyone concerned with the production, that spring was a happy, absorbing time, and an intensely creative time as well.

Sweet Bird would reach Broadway in a couple of years, and it would be his most substantial hit since *Cat,* but Williams would always think that somewhere between Miami and Broadway, something irretrievable was lost.

In Rome the previous summer he had written an original screenplay for Elia Kazan's Newtown Production Company, washing down Seconals with martinis to get his creative juices flowing. In this comedy about the Mississippi Delta he fused together two of his early one-act plays, *27 Wagons Full of Cotton* and *The Unsatisfactory Supper.* Years earlier, in their "Literary Factory," he and Clark Mills had laughed at the idea of a little man with a whip taking amorous advantage of a large, stupid woman. To this basic situation from *27 Wagons Full of Cotton,* he added the character of Aunt Rose Comfort, the aged relative who cooked supper but forgot to light the stove in *The Long Stay Cut Short,* or *The Unsatisfactory Supper.* In *Baby Doll,* as the new screenplay was called, Archie Lee Mehan emerged as a shiftless clod married to Baby Doll, his mindless child bride whom he has promised not to touch till she's "ready" for marriage, still some two years hence. When their furniture is repossessed, Archie Lee burns down his neighbor's cotton gin and then offers to gin the cotton for badly needed money. Silva Vaccaro, the Sicilian-American victim of the arson, suspects Archie Lee, but hires him anyway to gin the twenty-seven wagons full of cotton. When Archie Lee goes off, Vaccaro turns his attention to Baby Doll. They play a wild game of hide-and-seek (an early title) while Aunt Rose Comfort picks roses, "poems of nature." Later Vaccaro takes a nap in Baby Doll's crib and then cons her into admitting her husband's guilt for the arson.

It was a very funny film, and Williams' natural earthy humor is much in evidence. He thinks the script had a wanton hilarity which was never rightly or fully used in the film. *Baby Doll* opened in New York and caused an immediate furor. Mayor Robert Wagner's name had been erroneously used in connection with the Actors' Studio benefit showing, and Francis Cardinal Spellman personally took the pulpit of St. Patrick's Cathedral to denounce its "moral corrupting influence." Williams thinks that maybe Carroll Baker as Baby Doll did a little too much thumb sucking, but the film never struck him as anything but funny.

Through the years the one play that had never left Williams' writing desk was *Battle of Angels,* his first professionally produced work that had been such a disaster in Boston those many years ago. Through the years he had worked on

Williams paints for relaxation in a free, full-flowing style in light pastel colors. He paints in symbols, both real and unreal, frequently dealing with religious or allegorical subjects. He is posed here with his latest work, "The Faith of Gatsby's Last Summer." Other titles include "Le Tombe d'un Homme Inconnu," "In a Curtained Alcove," and "3 Nuts." In Key West he frequently contributes his work to various charities including the American Civil Liberties Union of Florida. The latest painting is interesting because it was painted at the time he was engrossed in *The Red Devil Battery Sign*, and recalls the Optometrist billboard in the opening pages of *The Great Gatsby*.

COLLECTION OF TENNESSEE WILLIAMS

Williams once appeared on BBC radio with Sir John Gielgud and confided to a friend that while it was supposed to be "conversation" he was nervous that the best lines would be given to Sir John. Gloria Swanson was considered of course for *The Roman Spring of Mrs. Stone* but it was thought that her brilliant success in *Sunset Boulevard* might raise unfair comparisons between the two films.

ARNOLD WEISSBURGER

New Orleans fascinated Williams. He explored the city from shacks along the river to the lovely homes and fountains in the Garden District. He liked it more than anything he'd seen in Europe. That winter, in 1938, the Vieux Carré became his spiritual home.

COURTESY OF GEORGE ROBISON BLACK

Peter Harvey's set for *Orpheus Descending* at the Coconut Grove Playhouse was a Williams favorite for which he sent a telegram of appreciation to the young designer. Owen Phillips directed Maureen Stapleton, Rip Torn and Nan Martin in a two-week limited engagement. During the technical rehearsal, a balky problem involving the storm projection caused an exasperated Williams to declare that "henceforth I shall confine myself to writing action involving kitchen curtains or flower arrangement."

PHOTO BY O.E. NELSON, COURTESY OF
PHILIP GILLIAN

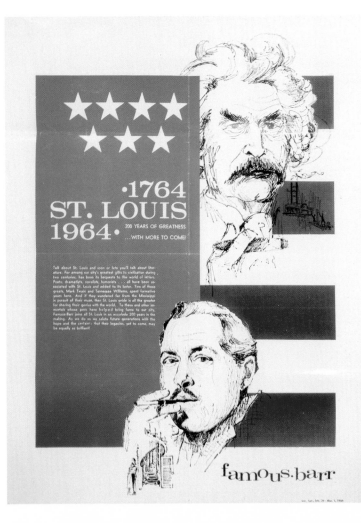

Williams has always disliked St. Louis ("the City of St. Pollution") because of his desperately unhappy years there, but the city honored him during its Bicentennial Celebration.

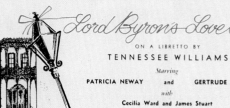

Following the disaster of *Battle of Angels* in Boston, Williams headed south for Key West in the winter of 1940, following a path well trod by so many earlier American artists, writers and poets.

The last photograph taken of Frieda Lawrence in her Taos, New Mexico, home. Williams always thought of her as a monument to the life force, almost a living embodiment of D. H. Lawrence's mystique. He would visit her many times before her death in 1956, and she would write a preface to *I Rise in Flame, Cried the Phoenix*, his short play about the death of D. H. Lawrence.

REPRODUCED BY PERMISSION, PATRICIA CLINE HOLMES

THEATRE DU
RIDEAU DE BRUXELLES

Sixième année   Animateur : Claude ÉTIENNE

TOUS LES SOIRS à 20 h. 15 - DERNIERE le 9 JANVIER
Sauf les 22 et 31 déc. - Matinées à 15 h. les 25, 26 déc., 2 et 9 janvier
24 Décembre : Soirée de REVEILLON à 20 h. 15

75ᵉ SALLE DU PETIT THEATRE **75ᵉ**
IRREVOCABLES DERNIERES

LA MENAGERIE
DE VERRE

VENDREDI 31 DECEMBRE à 20 h. 15

REVEILLON DE L'AN
SALLE DE MUSIQUE DE CHAMBRE
LE CHEF-D'ŒUVRE DE L'ESPRIT FRANÇAIS

AMPHITRYON 38

Comédie en 3 actes de Jean GIRAUDOUX

➤ SOIREES DE REVEILLON : PRIX ORDINAIRE DES PLACES ◄
Bureau de location tous les jours ouvrables de 11 à 17 h. (Tél. 11.13.75) du

PALAIS DES BEAUX-ARTS

Imp. F. FERRANT, 11, Av. Clemenceau, Brux.

THEATRE CHARLES DE ROCHEFORT
64, Rue du Rocher   Direction : Mary GRANT   Métro : Villiers - Saint-Lazare

TOUS LES SOIRS A 21 h. (Sauf Jeudi) MATINEE : DIMANCHE A 15 h.
A PARTIR DU 20 MARS
POUR 15 REPRESENTATIONS SEULEMENT

EVE WATKINSON
ARTHUR KLEIN

dans

THE GLASS MENAGERIE
(LA MENAGERIE DE VERRE)

de

TENNESSEE WILLIAMS
in English - En Anglais

Mise en scène de ARTHUR KLEIN
Musique de PAUL BOWLES

avec

GRACE CHAPMAN
JACK ARONSON

Une œuvre délicate ! Un merveilleux divertissement !
One of America's most significant and sensitive plays !

★

PLACES de 300 à 1.000 FRANCS
Location : Théâtre, Durand, 4, Place de la Madeleine Agences - Réductions Etudiants J. M. F.

the harvard advocate presents

Tennessee Williams

reading from his plays

introduced by Elliot Norton
april 19   8:30 pm
sanders theater

tickets 1.20 · 1.80 · 2.40
at the coop · mandrake
or tr6 6721

Williams has always considered himself primarily a poet, and he credits a poetry reading with starting him on the road to recovery in the late 1960s.

RIDEAU DE BRUXELLES
NEUVIEME ANNEE
Directeur : CLAUDE ETIENNE

PALAIS DES BEAUX-ARTS
SALLE DE MUSIQUE DE CHAMBRE

DU 7 AU 20 JANVIER 1952 (SAUF LES 11 - 14 ET 18)
Tous les soirs à 20 h. 15 - Matinée les dimanches 13 et 20 à 15 h.

CREATION SUR LE CONTINENT
de la dernière pièce de
TENNESSEE WILLIAMS
adaptation française de
RAYMOND GEROME

LA ROSE TATOUÉE

avec, par ordre alphabétique

Paul ANRIEU   Gaston DERBLAY   Pierre MOTTE
Denyse BERGER   Michel GHAYE   Denyse PERIEZ
Anne CARPRIAU   Suzanne JEHAN   Paul SAUSSUS
Nelly CORBUSIER   Nicole LEPAGE   Juliette VERBO
Christiane DAILLY   Louise MONY   Irène VERNAL
                                          Eve WINTER

Mise en scène de
MAURICE VANEAU
supervisée avec l'accord du Théâtre National, par
RAYMOND GEROME
Régie : André DEPREZ
DECOR DE EMILE LANC

Du 8 au 20, sauf les 17 et 18, tous les soirs à 20 h. 15 - Matinée les 13 et 20 à 15 h. - Petit Théâtre
LA MENAGERIE DE VERRE

Bureau de location du Palais des Beaux-Arts, 23, rue Ravenstein (de 11 à 17 heures)
Location par téléphone : 44.41.29 - 11.79.55

Affiches F. TYTGAT, Ch. d'Alsemberg, 258, Bruxelles — Téléphone : 43.66.41

it on and off, shifting the nuance, changing some of the more obvious Christian symbolism, but keeping it essentially the story of a wild-spirited poet/troubadour who wanders into the conventional hell of a small southern town seeking purification from early corruption only to end up crucified/destroyed by the townspeople/furies for bringing love to a sex-starved woman. The new version of the play contained approximately 75 percent new writing, and because it conformed more literally to the Greek legend, he called it *Orpheus Descending.*

This play is a key work to understanding Tennessee Williams. The poets of the world destroyed by the furies is a conflict basic to his imagination. *Orpheus Descending* is a protest against the cruelty of human beings and against a society that destroys its nonconformists.

The play ran a disappointing sixty-eight performances on Broadway, but critics noted that even secondhand Williams was more exhilarating than most of the plays that turn up there. They also felt that *Orpheus* lacked the beauty necessary to convey such brutal truths convincingly. Most European critics were lukewarm toward the play, but interestingly enough, *Orpheus Descending* ran for seven years in repertory in the Soviet Union. A movie sale would bring Italy's Anna Magnani back to America, and she would co-star with Marlon Brando in the film, renamed *The Fugitive Kind.*

The failure of *Orpheus Descending* only added to the accumulation of problems which had plagued Williams for years, and the symptoms of claustrophobia, hypochondria, alcoholism, and his longtime fear of suffocation led him to undergo Freudian analysis in New York. Interest in his analysis led him to read deeply about the subject, and he came to believe that the key to his problem was infantile omnipotence—anger at an indifferent world. His doctor disagreed and urged him to break off his relationship with Frank Merlo, something Williams refused to do, saying, "How could I?" His life was built around Merlo.

During the analysis he came quite naturally to reflect on his sister, Rose, and upon the lobotomy which had destroyed any hope for her eventual recovery. From out of this grew *Suddenly Last Summer,* a macabre study of guilt and atonement in which Williams imposed his personal interpretation on a surrealistic impression of hell. Through the story of Sebastian Venable, a poet who corrupts others in his search for purity, he dramatized his vision of a cannibalistic universe.

Williams showed the new play to his friend Herbert Machiz, who liked it and made immediate arrangements to direct it in one of Manhattan's newest Off-Broadway houses. It was presented with *Something Unspoken,* a short curtain raiser about two women in a tense love/hate relationship under the collective title *Garden District. Suddenly Last Summer* became the most talked-about new play of the season. Both the *Tribune* and the New York *Times* gave it rave notices. Williams had expected to be run out of New York.

Since its first production at Studio "M" in Miami, Williams had continued to work on *Sweet Bird of Youth.* His growing preoccupation with time passing and the problem of facing death in life was becoming increasingly important to him, and in *Sweet Bird,* Time became an antagonist. And it had all the Williams touches: the play opens on Easter Sunday morning, church bells ring, and the play is filled with echoes of resurrection, purification, corruption, and atonement. His penchant for mixing classical Greek mythology with Christian symbolism is evident throughout the play. *Sweet Bird* was unanimously praised by all seven New York critics, and MGM purchased the film rights. It was his most substantial success since *Cat on a Hot Tin Roof.*

For the production of his first comedy, *Period of Adjustment,* Williams chose the relaxed atmosphere of the Coconut Grove Playhouse, where Owen Phillips directed the story of two neurotic couples trying to make a go of marriages not made in heaven. The play unfolds their special sex problems on Christmas Eve in a place called High Point built over a cavern, an allusion suggested by his mother's house in St. Louis. Although the play marked a change in both mood and theme for Williams, it still concerned the same frustrated men and women who had appeared in his work for twenty years and grew out of his theory of idealism in conflict with reality, or sex and love, of the loneliness and the need for meaningful communication between people. When Elia Kazan backed out of the New York production, George Roy Hill directed the comedy to generally enthusiastic notices.

The decade of the 1950s had been a busy, productive time for Williams, and he would write one more play just as it ended. For *The*

Night of the Iguana, he turned to the lush setting of the Costa Verde above the rain forest and the still water beach he had known in Mexico during his trip there in 1940. To a small hotel run by an amorous landlady who is seeking a more permanent lover than her two Mexican houseboys comes the Reverend T. Lawrence Shannon, a defrocked minister who is unable to find any meaning in his life. Into this world wanders a gallant spinster with a fighting spirit. She accompanies her grandfather, the world's oldest living poet, who is racing death to finish a poem. The play abounds in long, compelling statements about life, the sort of confessionals in which Williams excels. In his inability to accept God, Shannon is as trapped as the iguana tied up beneath the porch. *The Night of the Iguana* is a bleak portrait of people unable to communicate with each other and of man's search for God.

Williams won his fourth New York Drama Critics' Award for the play, and if it represented a high point in his professional career, it also marked the beginning of a low point in his personal life. He would write other plays, and they would be produced with varying degrees of critical success, but as the decade of the 1960s wore on, the years ahead would see his personal world begin to collapse and disintegrate. Following the death of Frank Merlo, his dependence on drugs to alleviate his depression and loneliness would reach crisis proportions. Williams would come, in the middle of his life, to his own dark wood where the straight way was lost.

"I still believe that the open country of Mexico is the most beautiful country in the world, and I have seen a great deal of the world."

MEXICAN NATIONAL TOURIST OFFICE

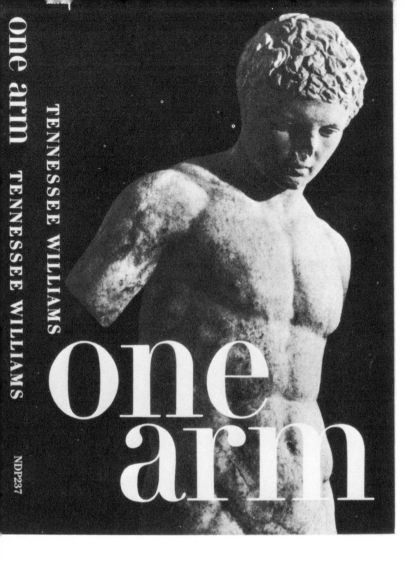

Williams' first published book of stories, brought out in an expensive private edition by New Directions, established him as a writer of offbeat talent.

New Directions

Returning to the States from Mexico, Williams was detained overnight in Laredo while his trunkful of manuscripts were read by a Mexican girl-censor. When he called for them, *One Arm* was missing and an enraged Williams threw a wild scene for which he was nearly jailed and during which he declared that the manuscript was his life's work and that existence without it was unthinkable. The mini-drama ended when they calmed him with whiskey and found the story intact in his trunk.

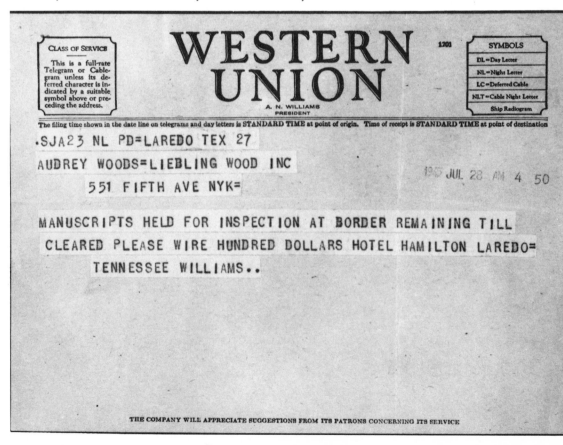

 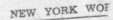

THE PLAYBILL

FOR THE BOOTH THEATRE

Montgomery Clift was one of the fastest-rising young actors on Broadway in 1945. While Williams thinks that its an oversimplification of the problems of a tragically complex artist whom he never quite understood except on stage, he suspects that Monty's decline began with the astonishing advent of Marlon Brando in *Streetcar*.

OPENING-NIGHT NOTICE, YOU TOUCHED ME!

Theater
By Burton Rascoe

'You Touched Me'
a First-Rate Comedy

At long last the new season has produced a play which I c recommend to one and all, wholeheartedly and without serious re ervations, as a work of art, edification and entertainment. It is "Y Touched Me," a comedy by Tennessee Williams and Donald Win ham, based upon a short story by D. H. Lawrence, which opened at t Booth last night. It is adult comedy, provoking many hearty laughs. It is also a vigorous and subtle affirmation of the life-spirit, or, as Bergson called it, the elan vital.

As anyone who is familiar with the work of the late D. H. Lawrence knows, that Nottinghamshire coal miner's son, who became one of the most discussed writers of modern times, was obsessed with the idea that a false sense of righteousness and morality (induced by the preponderance of women over men in the United Kingdom) had not only made British middleclass women frigid but had given them such a whip-hand over men as to devitalize them.

Lawrence's short story, from which the title and the idea of the present play are derived, was only a minor skirmish in Lawrence's militant crusade to free British women from the fear of giving normal expression to their humane and natural emotions a n d to emancipate British men from the bleak sort of matriarchy which, Lawrence contended, their women-folk had imposed upon them, stifling their masculinity and killing their spirit of adventure.

"You Touched Me," as a play, is about the final triumph of a bibulous old former sea captain over the domination of himself, his daughter, and his adopted son, by a self-righteous and mentally sadistic spinster sister. Although the home in which she lived and ruled and the income on which she thrived in piety and pretention were her brother's, the unwed female had got the hearty buckeroo under her thumb after he had gone on a binge in the Caribbean, foundered his ship, and suffered the dishonor of losing his skipper's certificate. Thereafter, of course, he was hers to pity, suffer martyrdom for, take care of and — keep drunk, by constantly telling him what a disgraceful sot he was.

The return, on a brief furlough, of the waif the s k i p p e r had brought up, revives in the old boy a will to fight for his own survival as a free individual. His chance comes when he senses that a deep love has sprung up between his

'You Touched Me!'

By Tennessee Williams and Donald Winham, based on a short story by D. Lawrence, staged by Guthrie McClintic; se by Motley; produced by Mr. McClintic association with Lee Shubert at the Boo Theatre, Sept. 25 with the following cast:

Matilda Rockley	Marianne Stewa
Emmie	Catherine Willar
Phoebe	Norah Howar
Hadrian	Montgomery Clif
Cornelius Rockley	Edmund Gwen
Rev. Guiford Melton	Neil Fitzgera
Muscle Dancer	Wauna Pa
Policeman	Freeman Hammon

foster-son and his daughter — love thwarted, for pecuniary well as more obscure reasons, the girl's spinster aunt, who h hade a zombie out of the girl. T skipper's greatest difficulty lies overcoming the fears and re cences that have been instilled the boy and the girl by the harp

The play offers a field day f Edmund Gwenn, as the lovable o toper. He squeezes every bit juice out of the characterizatio reaching a high point in his na ration of the time when, after b ing long at sea and in his cur he responded to the amorous a vances of a flirtatious lady po poise. He had tears of laught pouring down my cheeks at th and at several other points.

Catherine Willard, playing som what the same role she handled superbly in "The Deep Mrs. Sykes does a grand job as the harp Niel Fitzgerald is quite satisfa tory as the ecclesiastical neut and Marianne Stewart did fair well as the spiritless girl; b Montgomery Clift after his pr vious performances was a distin disappointment to me. He has drive, no variation in tone, spirit; he has only a trick of sta ing with a hurt look and makir at the same time, a wry twist wi his mouth, which was all rig when he was a disillusioned se dier in "The Searching Wind," a psychoneurotic in "Foxhole the Parlor," but it has no relati to the character called for by t text of the play. Mr. Clift's si pering listlessness is the only fat I can find with Guthrie McCli tic's direction of the play.

A bill of Williams' one-act plays was presented on Nantucket Island the summer of 1946. Earlier that summer he had read several of them at a local art gallery, asking only for a couple of scarce sugar coupons in pay. He received enough to last the entire summer.

Carson McCullers arrived on Nantucket Island looking surprisingly like Frankie Adams, her heroine in *The Member of the Wedding.* She wore blue jeans, a baseball cap, and a crooked smile. Williams has since recalled their first meeting:

> . . . almost immediately after Carson and the sun appeared on the island, I relinquished the romantic notion that I was a dying artist. My various psychosomatic symptoms were forgotten. There was warmth and light in the house, the odor of good cooking and the nearly-forgotten sight of clean dishes and silver. Also there was some coherent talk for a change. Long evening conversations over hot rum and tea, the reading of poetry aloud, bicycle rides and wanderings along moonlit dunes, and one night there was a marvelous display of the Aurora Borealis, great quivering sheets of white, radiance sweeping over the island and the ghostly white fisherman's houses and fences. That night and that mysterious phenomenon will always be associated in my mind with the discovery of our friendship, or rather, more precisely, with the spirit of this newfound friend, who seemed as curiously and beautifully unworldly as that night itself.

COURTESY OF THE GOTHAM BOOK MART

Stairs to the Roof received its only performance at the Pasadena Playhouse in 1947.

A production scene from *Stairs to the Roof* showing a pantomime with recitation (Beauty and the Beast) in the play-within-a-play toward the end of the third act in this fantasy about his life in the shoe warehouse.

PHOTO BY WES WELAND, COLLECTION OF TENNESSEE WILLIAMS

Pasadena
PLAYHOUSE NEWS
"STAIRS TO THE ROOF"
FEBRUARY 26, 1947

Williams lived in a second-floor apartment in Dick Orme's house on the corner of St. Peter and Royal streets in New Orleans during the winter of 1947. Below him two street-cars, Desire and Cemeteries, ran up and down the Royal Street tracks. Their symbolism, in a happy mixture of Freud and classical Greek mythology, suggested a new title for *The Poker Night*.

COLLECTION OF TENNESSEE WILLIAMS

Blanche
They told me to take a streetcar named *Desire*, and then transfer to one called *Cemeteries* and ride six blocks and get off at—Elysian Fields!
        —*A Streetcar Named Desire*

COURTESY OF THE NEW ORLEANS POWER AND LIGHT CO. INC.

Marion Black Vaccaro, widowed now, lived in the Pontal-ba building in the Vieux Carré, where she entertained Williams and a touring cast of *The Glass Menagerie*. Always devoted friends, they had become each other's favorite traveling companion. He called her "Sister"; she called him "Tommy." He would dedicate *Orpheus Descending* to her. For several years after leaving Smith College, Marion was a member of the Ziegfeld family as tutor companion to Patricia, the only child of Florenz and Billie Burke Ziegfeld.

COURTESY OF GEORGE ROBISON BLACK

Williams and his grandfather became a familiar sight on South Beach in Key West during the summer of 1947. Williams lavished attention and consideration on the old gentleman; called him "that ancient charmer" and indulged him by selecting only those dining places which still served on table linen. Although increasingly hard of hearing and nearly blind now, Dr. Dakin loved traveling with his grandson and approved of everything he wrote.

COURTESY OF ROBERT A. MORGAN, JR.

Williams seemed predestined to collaborate with Elia Kazan. A disciple of the Stanislavsky Moscow school, the dynamic director shared with Williams the same interest in experimental technique. He gave to Williams the writer a great feeling of sympathy which the playwright needed and appreciated. *A Streetcar Named Desire* established them as Broadway's hottest combination, and they would work together on *Camino Real, Cat on a Hot Tin Roof, Sweet Bird of Youth,* and the film *Baby Doll*. Williams always enjoyed working with Kazan.

COLLECTION OF TENNESSEE WILLIAMS, PORTRAIT BY G. MAILLARD KESSLERE, B.P.

Jessica Tandy was first mentioned for *Streetcar* by her husband, actor/producer/director Hume Cronyn when he stopped in to thank Audrey Wood for permitting his Actor's Lab to perform *Portrait of a Madonna* without royalty. Kazan offered her the role of Blanche, but to give Williams a chance to see her, Cronyn briefly revived his West Coast production. Together with Audrey Wood and Irene Selznick, Williams took the Super Chief and caught her performance. She was as sensational as he'd heard. After he saw her, he said, "It was instantly apparent to me that Jessica was Blanche."

On the porch of the Atlantic House in Provincetown during the summer of 1947, Williams met Frank Philip Merlo, who was destined to become, for fourteen years, the most important person in his life. Merlo's direct, straightforward manner would do much to ease Williams' shyness with strangers.

Sketch of Frank Merlo

LITTLE HORSE
For F. M.

Mignon he was or *mignonette*
avec les yeux plus grands que lui.
My name for him was Little Horse.
I fear he had no name for me.

I came upon him more by plan
than accidents appear to be.
Something started or something stopped
and there I was and there was he.

And then it rained but Little Horse
had brought along his *parapluie.*
Petit cheval it kept quite dry
till he divided it with me.

For it was late and I was lost
when Little Horse enquired of me,
What has a bark but cannot bite?
And I was right. It was a tree.

Mignon he is or *mignonette*
avec les yeux plus grands que lui.
My name for him is Little Horse.
I wish he had a name for me.

74

Rehearsals for *Streetcar* on the roof of the New Amsterdam Theater were a happy time for Brando, Karl Malden, Jessica Tandy, and Kim Hunter, who were aware of a superior script. Kazan welcomed Williams at all rehearsals and even had him demonstrate the old Mexican woman with the flowers, but Williams was beset with doubts. He thought the play would be a certain failure.

JOSEPH ABELES STUDIO

Marlon Brando was just about the best-looking young man Williams had ever seen. He hitchhiked to the Cape, repaired William's broken toilet, got the lights working, and then, with Williams cueing him, gave an electrifying reading in a role originally thought of for John Garfield. Margo Jones, in a burst of enthusiasm, exclaimed "I never heard a better reading in Texas." Brando would go on in Williams' opinion to become the world's greatest living actor.

JOSEPH ABELES STUDIO

Irene Mayer Selznick, producer of *A Streetcar Named Desire*, had recently produced Arthur Laurent's *Heartsong*. That play didn't reach Broadway, but Audrey Wood was sufficiently impressed to offer her *Streetcar*.

The Poker Night by Thomas Hart Benton was commissioned by MGM's Louis B. Mayer as a surprise Christmas gift to his daughter, Irene Selznick. *Look* magazine wanted to photograph the cast of *Streetcar* posed like the painting. Jessica Tandy demurred, and the incident prompted an exchange of notes between her and Williams.

Dear Jessica:

I have been appointed intermediator in the delicate matter of persuading you to pose for a photographic duplication of the Thomas Hart Benton painting which our Lady Producer is to be surprised with at Christmas. I have seen a picture of the painting. It looks marvelous and of course Benton is a very outstanding painter. I can see how Blanche's dress, or lack of it, might offend you, but I am assured that you will not have to be so anatomical and I suppose the idea is an excellent piece of promotion. Myself I don't see it is vulgar, but I cannot swear that my sense of vulgarity is the most impeccable in the world.

Ever,

Tennessee

P.S. I believe Blanche would — after some initial protest,

November 2, 1948.

Dear Jessica:

Many, many thanks for your letter on the Benton picture. You are so right that it really makes me ashamed of having lent my casual support to the idea. What you say about Blanche suddenly recalls to me all of my original conception of the character and what it was to me, from which you, in your delineation, have never once drifted away in spite of what I now realize must have been a continual pressure: that unwillingness of audiences to share a more intricate and special and sensitive response to things; their desire to participate more safely, familiarly, in the responses of an animal nature. I have almost forgotten (perhaps under this same pressure) that it was Blanche whom I loved and respected and whom I wished to portray, though I have never, please believe me, forgotten the exact and tender and marvelously understanding way that you brought her to life. -- I have such a divided nature! Irreconciliably divided. I look at Benton's picture and I see the strong things in it, its immediate appeal to the senses, raw, sensual, dynamic, and I forgot the play was really about those things which are opposed to that, the delicate half-approaches to something much finer. Yes, the Stanley side of it. Perhaps from the painter's point of view that was inevitable. A canvas cannot depict two worlds very easily; or the tragic division of the human spirit; at least not a painter of Benton's realistic type. Well, believe me, still more an admirer of the painting, but I am still an admirer of yours for seeing and feeling about it more clearly than I did at first, and I should have felt the same way.

With love,

Tennessee

Dear Tennessee:

You have the wrong impression of my objection to posing for a photographic duplicate of the Benton picture.

Eight times a week, and to progressively less sensitive audiences, I have to make clear Blanche's intricate and complex character -- her background -- her pathetic elegance -- her indomitable spirit -- her innate tenderness and honesty -- her untruthfulness or manipulation of the truth -- her inevitable tragedy.

My protagonist Stanley -- my executioner as you put it -- is comparatively simple and easy for an audience to understand.

The setting is a wonderful mixture of the qualities of both these characters -- decayed elegance and sheer unadulterated guts.

I share your admiration for Benton as a painter, but in this painting he has chosen to paint, it seems to me, the Stanley side of the picture. Even in the set, you are more conscious of telegraph poles than scrolled ironwork.

There has always been a part of the audience who obviously expects a sexy, salacious play. I don't want to do anything which will lead future audiences to think that they are going to see sex in the raw, as it were.

FIRST NIGHT AT THE THEATRE

IN THE PLAY: *"What do you think you are, a pair of queens? Remember what Huey Long said—every man is a king and I'm king around here so don't forget it!"*—Marlon Brando to Jessica Tandy (center) and Kim Hunter.

By BROOKS ATKINSON

Tennessee Williams has brought us a superb drama, "A Streetcar Named Desire," which was acted at the Ethel Barrymore last evening. And Jessica Tandy gives a superb performance as rueful heroine whose misery Mr. Williams is tenderly recording. This must be one of the most perfect marriages of acting and playwriting. For the acting and playwriting are perfectly blended in a limpid performance, and it is impossible to tell where Miss Tandy begins to give form and warmth to the mood Mr. Williams has created.

Like "The Glass Menagerie," the new play is a quietly woven study of intangibles. But to this observer it shows deeper insight and represents a great step forward toward clarity. And it reveals Mr. Williams as a genuinely poetic playwright whose knowledge of people is honest and thorough and whose sympathy is profoundly human.

* * *

"A Streetcar Named Desire" is history of a gently reared Mississippi young woman who invents an artificial world to mask the hideousness of the world she has to inhabit. She comes to live with her sister, who is married to a rough-and-ready mechanic and inhabits two dreary rooms in a squalid neighborhood. Blanche—for that is her name—has delusions of grandeur, talks like an in-

A STREETCAR NAMED DESIRE, a play in three acts, by Tennessee Williams. Staged by Elia Kazan; scenery and lighting by Jo Mielziner; costumes by Lucinda Ballard; produced by Irene M. Selznick. At the Barrymore Theatre.

Negro Woman	Gee Gee James
Eunice Hubbel	Peg Hillias
Stanley Kowalski	Marlon Brando
Harold Mitchell (Mitch)	Karl Malden
Stella Kowalski	Kim Hunter
Steve Hubbel	Rudy Bond
Blanche du Bois	Jessica Tandy
Pablo Gonzales	Nick Dennis
A Young Collector	Vito Christi
Mexican Woman	Edna Thomas
A Strange Woman	Ann Dere
A Strange Man	Richard Garrick

tellectual snob, buoys herself up with gaudy dreams, spends most of her time primping, covers things that are dingy with things that are bright and flees reality.

To her brother-in-law she is an unforgiveable liar. But it is soon apparent to the theatregoer that in Mr. Williams' eyes she is one of the dispossessed whose experience has unfitted her for reality; and although his attitude toward her is merciful, he does not spare her or the playgoer. For the events of "Streetcar" lead to a painful conclusion which he does not try to avoid. Although Blanche cannot face the truth, Mr. Williams does in the most imaginative and perceptive play he has written.

* * *

Since he is no literal dramatist and writes in none of the conventional forms, he presents the theatre with many problems. Under Elia Kazan's sensitive but concrete direction, the theatre has solved them admirably. Jo Mielziner has provided a beautifully lighted sin-

gle setting that lightly sketches the house and the neighborhood. In this shadowy environment the performance is a work of great beauty.

Miss Tandy has a remarkably long part to play. She is hardly ever off the stage, and when she is on stage she is almost constantly talking — chattering, dreaming aloud, wondering, building enchantments out of words. Miss Tandy is a trim, agile actress with a lovely voice and quick intelligence. Her performance is almost incredibly true. For it does seem almost incredible that she could understand such an elusive part so thoroughly and that she can convey it with so many shades and impulses that are accurate, revealing and true.

* * *

The rest of the acting is also of very high quality indeed. Marlon Brando as the quick-tempered, scornful, violent mechanic; Karl Malden as a stupid but wondering suitor; Kim Hunter as the patient though troubled sister—all act not only with color and style but with insight.

By the usual Broadway standards, "A Streetcar Named Desire" is too long; not all those words are essential. But Mr. Williams is entitled to his own independence. For he has not forgotten that human beings are the basic subject of art. Out of poetic imagination and ordinary compassion he has spun a poignant and luminous story.

The critics admired everything about *Streetcar:* the lighting, the direction, the acting, even the writing. It would run 855 performances on Broadway and become the first American play to win all three major awards: The Pulitzer Prize, The New York Drama Critics Circle Award, and The Donaldson Award. Williams donated the Pulitzer Prize money to the University of Missouri for a scholarship in graduate journalism.

The 1949 production of *Streetcar* in Gothenburg, Sweden, starred Kairn Koali as Blanche du Bois.

When *Streetcar* director Elia Kazan needed a few ad-libs to cover the initial entrance of Stanley and Mitch before the first line of the play, Williams wrote these in fifteen minutes.

COURTESY OF THE WALTER HAMPDEN MEMORIAL LIBRARY, PLAYERS CLUB

IRENE M. SELZNICK
COMPANY

TO_____
FROM_____
MEMO:

Ad libs Scene One: Eunice and Geegee at beginning:

IRENE M. SELZNICK
COMPANY

TO_____
FROM_____
MEMO:

Geegee: She says St. Cristopher would send out his dog to lick her and when he did she'd

IRENE M. SELZNICK
COMPANY

TO_____
FROM_____
MEMO:

feel an icy cold wave all up an' down her. Well, that night when— (men enter)

IRENE M. SELZNICK
COMPANY

TO_____
FROM_____
MEMO:

Stanley: —no pressure— down to 15! Mitch: Bearings burnt out? St. Hey, Stella.

BLANCHE

I don't want realism. I want magic! Yes, yes, magic! I try to give that to people. I misrepresent things to them. I don't tell truth, I tell what *ought* to be truth. And if that is sinful, then let me be damned for it!—*Don't turn the light on!*

STANLEY
What does it cost for a string of fur-pieces like that?
BLANCHE
Why those were a tribute from an admirer of mine!
STANLEY
He must have had a lot of—admiration!

BLANCHE
Whoever you are—I have always depended on the kindness of strangers.

Ethel Barrymore Theatre

Barrymore Theatre Corporation

FIRE NOTICE: The exit indicated by a red light and sign nearest to the seat you occupy is the shortest route to the street. In the event of fire please do not run—WALK TO THAT EXIT.
Frank J. Quayle,
FIRE COMMISSIONER

Thoughtless persons annoy patrons and distract actors and endanger the safety of others by lighting matches during the performance. Lighting of matches in theatres during the performance or at intermissions violates a city ordinance and renders the offender liable to a summons.

THE · PLAYBILL · A · WEEKLY · PUBLICATION · OF · PLAYBILL · INCORPORATED

Week beginning Monday, November 22, 1948   •   Matinees Wednesday and Saturday

IRENE M. SELZNICK

presents

ELIA KAZAN'S PRODUCTION OF

A STREETCAR NAMED DESIRE

by TENNESSEE WILLIAMS

Directed by MR. KAZAN

with JESSICA TANDY
MARLON BRANDO

KIM HUNTER   KARL MALDEN

Scenery and Lighting by   Costumes Designed by
Jo Mielziner   Lucinda Ballard

"And so it was I entered the broken world
To trace the visionary company of love, its voice
An instant in the wind (I know not whither hurled)
But not for long to hold each desperate choice."
—The Broken Tower by Hart Crane

Light on the palate
Light on the purse

Mount Vernon BRAND
WHISKEY · A BLEND

LIGHT on the palate

LIGHT on the purse

86 Proof — 72½% Grain Neutral Spirits.
National Distillers Products Corp., New York, N.Y.

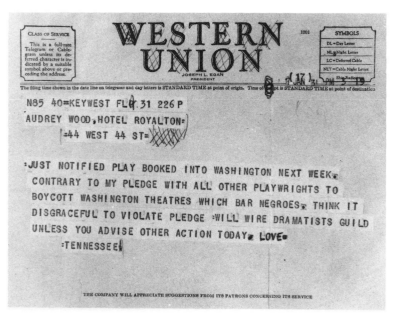

Williams has never forgiven himself for once imitating some neighborhood children at the age of four, and calling his black nurse "Nigger." It left him with a strong sense of abhorrence against discrimination of any kind.

Jean Cocteau's production of *Streetcar* in Paris created a storm of criticism. Williams watched the great Arletty as Blanche with Yves Vincent as Stanley during the rape scene in amazement as near-naked black dancers writhed behind a scrim. A letter from Lillian Gish (to whom he had dedicated *Portrait of a Madonna*) had forewarned him of the aberrant production.

Williams, who had inadvertently dressed like a waiter, met Clifton Webb at the Hollywood party given by producer Charles Feldman to celebrate his purchase of *Streetcar*. The decorations included an ice menagerie which melted as the evening progressed. Webb observed the water trickling onto the floor and told Williams that "Lolly must be having trouble with her kidneys again."

COLLECTION OF TENNESSEE WILLIAMS

In Brighton, England, Helen Hayes had warned Williams that *The Glass Menagerie* was in trouble, and he made it a point to miss the London opening. When he saw the production en route home from Europe, he agreed with her. His adverse criticism of Miss Hayes' acting ability may have been influenced by her published comments concerning her intense dislike of *The Glass Menagerie*.

In Rome, Williams bought a jeep from an American GI. In spite of its defective muffler, he cruised about Rome all night, driving drunkenly past windblown fountains till he was soaked. He and Gore Vidal took fun trips to Sorrento and Amalfi. Years later he would nearly kill himself in a white Jaguar. Noël Coward once leaped out of his Buick Roadmaster, calling it "a death trap." Williams, at best, is a highly erratic driver.

COLLECTION OF TENNESSEE WILLIAMS

Williams attended a reception for the visiting Sitwells at the Gotham Book Mart in New York in 1948. Grouped around the Sitwells, who are seated center, are, left foreground, seated, William Rose Benet, behind him, Stephen Spender, Horace Gregory, and his wife, Marya Zaturenska. Behind Osbert Sitwell are Williams, Richard Eberhart, Gore Vidal, Jose Garcia Villa, W. H. Auden on stepladder, Elizabeth Bishop, Marianne Moore. Seated on the right are Randall Jarrell, Delmore Schwartz. Seated center on floor, Charles Henri Ford.

GOTHAM BOOK MART, COURTESY OF ANDREAS BROWN

Dear Audrey —

I'm afraid it was a mistake for me to work so long on this play. The material is simply not sufficiently theatrical and no amount of re-working seems to overcome that defect. However I would like this version typed up — to give at least the illusion of completion, so I will feel free to go on with something else.

Please send copies (typed) to Me & Mary Hunter & Margo — don't read it yourself till it is typed.

It may be something I can resurrect later on.

I am also sending you the synopsis of the play (in first draft), which I will do next, (I hope!)

Love — 10

An early letter to Audrey Wood concerning *Summer and Smoke*.

The first New York production of *Summer and Smoke* was directed by Margo Jones and starred Margaret Phillips and Todd Andrews. Margo had produced an earlier version of the play in her Dallas Theatre '47 (a version which Brooks Atkinson called "unbearably lucid") but delayed the Broadway production one year because of *Streetcar*.

THE DALLAS DAILY NEWS

Miss Alma, in a scene from the Brazilian production of *Summer and Smoke*, lives out her long, lonely, wistful martyrdom of the sexually repressed in the shadow of Eternity, a fountain which broods over the play symbolic of spirit as the impenetrable body of stone with ice water for blood. "Alma" is Spanish for "soul," and this play is Williams' most complete interpretation of the South.

"Early Sorrow".

The angel of the fountain, backed by a deep green ~~massive palm~~ *palmetto leaves* tree, at dusk of an evening in May in the first few years of this century.

ALMA as a child of ten comes into the scene; middy blouse and ribboned braids. She already has the dignity of an adult: there is a quality of extraordinary delicacy and tenderness, or spirituality in her, which must set her distinctly apart from other children. She has a habit of holding her hands, one cupped under the other in a way similar to that of receiving the wafer at Holy Communion. This is a habit that will remain with her as an adult. She stands like that in front of the stone angel for a few moments; then bends to drink at the fountain. While she is bent at the fountain

JOHN, as a child, ENTERS. He shoots a pea-shooter at Alma's bent over back. She utters a startled cry and whirls about. He laughs.

It should be apparent in the scene between them that he is already a confirmed object of her adoration.)

John: Hi, Preacher's daughter. (HE ADVANCES TOWARD HER)

I been looking for you.

Alma: (hopefully) You have?

John: Was it you that put them handkerchiefs on my desk?

Alma: (She smiles uncertainly)

John: Answer up!

Alma: - I put a box of handkerchiefs on your desk.

John: I figured it was you. - What was the idea, Miss Priss?

~~Alma: You needed them.~~

~~John:~~ Trying to make a fool of me?

Alma: Oh, no!

John Then what was the idea?

Alma: You have a bad cold and your nose has been running all week

---

Summer and Smoke originally had a prologue which introduced John and Alma as children. Williams later rewrote the play and called it *The Eccentricities of a Nightingale,* which omits the children altogether, a version he prefers.

NATIONAL·INSTITUTE
OF·ARTS·AND·LETTERS

IN·RECOGNITION·OF·DISTINGUISHED·WORK·IN·THE·ARTS

TENNESSEE · WILLIAMS

WAS·ELECTED·TO·MEMBERSHIP·AT·THE·ANNUAL
MEETING·HELD·IN·THE·CITY·OF·NEW·YORK··1952

SECRETARY

PRESIDENT

AMES & ROLLINSON, N.Y.

NATIONAL INSTITUTE OF ARTS AWARD. In 1975, Williams would again be honored by the National Arts Club with the gold medal of honor for literature.

Director Jose Quintero would vindicate Williams' faith in *Summer and Smoke* with his Circle in the Square production in 1952. He would later perform a similar service for *Camino Real.* These Off-Broadway productions were important early plays in the years when this vital force in the American theatre was just beginning its most dramatic decade.

JOSEPH ABELES STUDIO

Geraldine Page re-created her unforgettable Circle in the Square characterization of Miss Alma in the Hal Wallis film with the late Lawrence Harvey. Blanche du Bois may be Williams' greatest character, but Miss Alma is his favorite.

Williams, Merlo, and Paul Bowles toured North Africa during a trip characterized by wild dashes across various frontiers and the near loss of his Buick Roadmaster when the brakes failed. They finally journeyed to Rome and joined friends of Bowles.

In Rome, Williams and Merlo met Janet Flanner, the *Genet* of the *New Yorker*'s "Letter from Paris," and her friend Natalia Danesi Murray. He would love and admire them always. The Italian press, much to Williams' amusement, consistently referred to Merlo as his "interpreter."

Later on this trip Merlo introduced Williams to Sicily. A grateful Williams would dedicate *The Rose Tattoo* "to Frank, in exchange for Sicily." Merlo, detained there after Williams had returned to Rome, wired him it was because of death and diarrhea among his relatives. Williams, who guessed that Merlo had at least fifty relatives in Sicily, observed that it must be death to have diarrhea in a country with so few flush toilets.

In Rome with Luchino Visconti, Williams discussed the noted producer's upcoming production of *Streetcar*—a production he would very much admire. If Williams looks perplexed, it's because throughout their meetings, Visconti constantly called him "Blanche."

The Roman Spring of Mrs. Stone was Jose Quintero's first film and Williams' first novel. The book made the American best-seller list and created a furor in Rome, where authorities were still smarting over Fellini's *La Dolce Vita,* which they hadn't found at all sweet. Their outrage over Williams' decadent story set in their own city prevented the film from being made there. Years later, Louis de Rochemont produced the film in England with Quintero directing Vivian Leigh, Warren Beatty, and Lotte Lenya (who stole the film and won an Academy Award nomination) and Jeremy Spenser, terribly miscast as the Roman who springs on Mrs. Stone. But the picture is Williams' favorite film of any of his work. He calls it "a living poem."

Marion Black Vaccaro, now living on Biscayne Bay near Coconut Grove in Miami, was a frequent visitor to Key West, where "Sloppy Joes" was a favorite spot for a night on the town. Williams would often repay her visits, always staying at the Towers Hotel in Miami, and spending long hours at the adjacent Robert Clay Hotel Pool. The nearby old section of Miami would become the setting for his short play, *The Frosted Glass Coffin*.

COURTESY OF GEORGE ROBISON BLACK

In Key West, Williams and Merlo bought a small restored Bahamian house from the local florist. The house was white with bright red shutters and the property sported a white picket fence and enough land to later accommodate a swimming pool, studio, and guest home.

COLLECTION OF TENNESSEE WILLIAMS

Williams built a modest studio near the kitchen end of his house, and promptly dubbed it "the mad house." He furnished it simply with a long workbench beneath a skylight, a haphazard bookcase at one end, and wall decorations of foreign broadsides of his plays. He works every morning wherever he is, but he works best here, and he carries the only key to the knobless door.

Photo by Don Pinder, Key West

Williams loved the raffish charm of Key West in those early years before the tourists discovered it. He traveled constantly, but Merlo held the fort during his absence, entertaining a wide circle of friends. Williams always thought that Frank could easily have been elected mayor of the city.

Don Pinder, Key West

When *The Rose Tattoo* opened at the Martin Beck Theatre it had gone through five drafts and three title changes. Original it was called *The Eclipse of May 29, 1919,* and then *Eclipse of the Sun.* Cheryl Crawford produced it after Irene Selznick turned it down, telling Williams that it was material for an opera, not a play.

Martin Beck Theatre

Operated by Martin Beck Theatre Corp.

302 West Forty-fifth Street

Louis A. Lotito, Managing Director

THE · PLAYBILL · A · WEEKLY · PUBLICATION · OF · PLAYBILL · INCORPORATED

Beginning Saturday Evening, February 3, 1951 • Matinees Wednesday and Saturday

CHERYL CRAWFORD
presents

THE ROSE TATTOO

by
TENNESSEE WILLIAMS
Directed by DANIEL MANN

Settings Designed by
BORIS ARONSON

Costumes Designed by
ROSE BOGDANOFF

Incidental Music by DAVID DIAMOND

Lighting by Charles Elson

Production Associate, Bea Lawrence

". . . the streams are in their beds like the cries of women
and this world has more beauty than a ram's skin painted red!"
T. S. Eliot's translation of ANABASIS

CAST
(In Order of Appearance)

SALVATORE	SALVATORE MINEO
VIVI	JUDY RATNER
BRUNO	SALVATORE TAORMINA
ASSUNTA	LUDMILLA TORETZKA
ROSA DELLE ROSE	PHYLLIS LOVE
SERAFINA DELLE ROSE	MAUREEN STAPLETON
ESTELLE HOHENGARTEN	SONIA SOREL
THE STREGA	DAISY BELMORE
GIUSEPPINA	ROSSANA SAN MARCO
PEPINA	AUGUSTA MERIGHI
VIOLETTA	VIVIAN NATHAN
MARIELLA	PENNY SANTON
TERESA	NANCY FRANKLIN
FATHER DE LEO	ROBERT CARRICART
DOCTOR	ANDREW DUGGAN
MISS YORKE	DORRIT KELTON
FLORA	JANE HOFFMAN
BESSIE	FLORENCE SUNDSTROM
JACK HUNTER	DON MURRAY
SALESMAN	EDDIE HYANS
ALVARRO MANGIACAVALLO	ELI WALLACH
MAN	DAVID STEWART
MAN	MARTIN BALSAM

SCENES OF THE PLAY

LOCALE: A village populated mostly by Sicilians somewhere along the Gulf Coast between New Orleans and Mobile.

Maureen Stapleton and Eli Wallach were both products of the Actors Studio in New York. Williams, who calls both Maureen Stapleton and Eli Wallach "two of our best performers, with the warmest sympathy and understanding," he takes credit for discovering her for the role of Serafina. The goat chase from *The Rose Tattoo* marked the stage debut of ten-year-old Sal Mineo (center). Goats were very much on Williams' mind during the Chicago tryout; he dreamed that something had gone wrong with the lighting, and all he could see on the stage was a big shaggy black goat with yellow eyes that seemed to be speaking all the lines. When the show hit the summer doldrums in New York and the goat and the guitar were about to be sacrificed in the name of economy, he had to insist that they both be retained in the play.

"The Rose Tattoo is the Dionysian element in human life, its mystery, its beauty, its significance. It is that glittering quicksilver. . . . It is the dissatisfaction with empiric evidence that makes the poet and the mystic, for it is the lyric as well as Bacchantic impulse, and although the goat is one of its most immemorial symbols, it must not be confused with mere sexuality. The element is higher and more distilled than that. Its purest form is probably manifested by children and birds in their rhapsodic moments of flight and play . . . the limitless world of the dream. It is the *rosa mystica*."

Playbill cast page, *Tattoo*

National Theatret

I aften kl. 20—22,30

Den tatoverte rosen

Skuespill i tre akter, ti scener av
TENNESSEE WILLIAMS

Oversatt av Petter Magnus
Regi: Gerda Ring
Dekorasjonen av Rahe Raheny
Kostymene ved Lita Prahl

*

Personene:

SERAFINA DELLE ROSE	Aase Bye
ROSA DELLE ROSE	Liv Strømsted
ALVARO MANGIACAVALLO	Jørn Ording
JACK HUNTER	Johan Sverre
FADER DE LEO	Henrik Børseth
ESTELLE HOHENGARTEN	Ella Hval
ASSUNTA	Alfhild Stormoen
FRØKEN YORKE	Aagot Nissen
FLORA	Ingeborg Steffens
BESSIE	Hilde Solheim
STREGA	Aagot Børseth
DOKTOREN	Wilfred Brenstrand
SELGEREN	Rolf Sand
PEPPINA	Eva Engelsborg
VIOLETTA	Aagot Sperati
GUISEPPINA	Bonne Gauguin
MARIELLA	Gerd Rivedal Wiik
TERESA	Inger Marie Andersen
EN SICILIANSK SANGER	Pelle Christensen

Første akt:
1. scene: Aften.
2. » : I gryingen, dagen etter.
3. » : Ved middagstider samme dag.
4. » : Tre år senere. En formiddag om våren.
5. » : Like etter.
6. » : To timer senere, samme dag.

Annen akt:
1. scene: To timer senere, samme dag.

Tredje akt:
1. scene: Om aftenen, samme dag.
2. » : Like før soloppgang neste dag.
3. » : Morgen.

10 minutters opphold mellom aktene

Kjøp teatrets presangkort.

Ordinære billettpriser
I prisen er innbefattet garderobeavgift

Orkesterplass	kr. 12,00	2nen losjerad, 1. benk . . . . . kr. 6,00
Parkett, 5 første benker	» 10,00	—»— 2., 3. og 4. benk . . » 5,00
—»— 3 øvrige benker	» 7,50	—»— øvrige benker . . . » 3,00
Parterre	» 6,00	Fremmedlosje . . . . . . » 60,00
1ste losjerad, 2 første benker	» 10,00	Fremmedlosje — enkeltbilletter . . » 10,00
—»— øvrige benker	» 7,50	

Billettkontoret åpnes: Hverdager kl. 9 form., søn- og helligdager kl. 12 form.
Forsalg 2 dager forut.
Ingen overpris med mindre annerledes er bekjentgjort.
Kjøpte eller bestilte billetter tas ikke tilbake.
Telefonbestillinger hverdager fra kl. 10, søn- og helligdager fra kl. 13.

Hansmann & Jensen — Oslo

97

Maureen Stapleton and Felice Orlandi in *27 Wagons Full of Cotton*, the original play from which Williams would write *Baby Doll*.

The Starr Boarding House in *This Property Is Condemned* is an excellent example of a "Tennessee Williams set"—a dilapidated house, faded elegance crumbling into ruin, lacey wicker furniture, rambling verandas, and wonderful names like Starr Boarding House all permeated by a poetic atmosphere of gentle decay. Such sets are peopled, of course, by "Tennessee Williams characters," life's losers and misfits, sad lost romantic southern ladies dressed in yesteryear's fashions, suffering from sterility and broken dreams, dwelling precariously in a genteel past that exists only in their confused minds, individuals lost in the complex, impersonal modern world.

On the road in Philadelphia with *Camino Real,* Williams found his neighbor Johnny Ray a delightful companion. He also found the audience reaction to his new play puzzling. After New York, he would always think the bad notices were meant to punish him for daring to be unconventional.

National Theatre

THE · PLAYBILL · A · WEEKLY · PUBLICATION · OF · PLAYBILL · INCORPORATED

Beginning, Thursday Evening, March 19, 1953 • Matinees Wednesday and Saturday

IN THE EVENT OF AN AIR RAID ALARM REMAIN IN YOUR SEATS AND OBEY THE INSTRUCTIONS OF THE MANAGEMENT—HERBERT R. O'BRIEN, DIRECTOR OF CIVIL DEFENSE.

CHERYL CRAWFORD and ETHEL REINER
in association with WALTER P. CHRYSLER, JR.
present

the ELIA KAZAN PRODUCTION of
SIXTEEN BLOCKS ON THE

CAMINO REAL

a new play

By TENNESSEE WILLIAMS

with

Eli Wallach	Jo Van Fleet	Joseph Anthony
Jennie Goldstein	Frank Silvera	Barbara Baxley

and

Hurd Hatfield

Direction by MR. KAZAN
Entire Production Designed by LEMUEL AYERS

Assistant to the Director, Anna Sokolow   Incidental Music by Bernardo Ségall
Production Associate, Anderson Lawler

CAST
(In Order of Appearances)

GUTMAN	FRANK SILVERA
SURVIVOR	GUY THOMAJAN
ROSITA	AZA BARD
1st OFFICER	HENRY SILVA
A GENTLEMAN OF FORTUNE	JOSEPH ANTHONY
LA MADRECITA DE LOS PERDIDOS	VIVIAN NATHAN
HER SON	ROLANDO VALDEZ
KILROY	ELI WALLACH
1st STREET CLEANER	NEHEMIAH PERSOFF
2nd STREET CLEANER	FRED SADOFF
ABDULLAH	ERNESTO GONZALEZ
A BUM IN A WINDOW	MARTIN BALSAM
A. RATT	MIKE GAZZO
THE LOAN SHARK	SALEM LUDWIG
THE BARON	DAVID J. STEWART
LOBO	RONNE AUL
2nd OFFICER	WILLIAM LENNARD
A GROTESQUE MUMMER	GLUCK SANDOR
A LADY OF LEGEND	JO VAN FLEET
LADY MULLIGAN	LUCILLE PATTON
WAITER	PAGE JOHNSON
A ROMANTIC POET	HURD HATFIELD
NAVIGATOR OF THE FUGITIVO	ANTONY VORNO
PILOT OF THE FUGITIVO	MARTIN BALSAM
MARKET WOMAN	CHARLOTTE JONES
2nd MARKET WOMAN	JOANNA VISCHER
STREET VENDOR	RUTH VOLNER
LORD MULLIGAN	PARKER WILSON
THE GYPSY	JENNIE GOLDSTEIN
HER DAUGHTER, ESMERALDA	BARBARA BAXLEY
NURSIE	SALEM LUDWIG
EVA	MARY GREY
THE INSTRUCTOR	DAVID J. STEWART
ASSISTANT INSTRUCTOR	PARKER WILSON
MEDICAL STUDENT	PAGE JOHNSON
AN ANCIENT KNIGHT	HURD HATFIELD

Street Vendors: Aza Bard, Ernesto Gonzalez, Charlotte Jones, Gluck Sandor, Joanna Vischer, Ruth Volner, Antony Vorno.

Guests: Martin Balsam, Mary Grey, Lucille Patton, Joanna Vischer, Parker Wilson.

Passengers: Mike Gazzo, Mary Grey, Page Johnson, Charlotte Jones, William Lennard, Salem Ludwig, Joanna Vischer, Ruth Volner.

At the Fiesta: Ronne Aul, Martin Balsam, Aza Bard, Mike Gazzo, Ernesto Gonzalez, Mary Grey, Charlotte Jones, William Lennard, Nehemiah Persoff, Fred Sadoff, Gluck Sandor, Joanna Vischer, Antony Vorno, Parker Wilson.

THE TIME AND PLACE: NOT SPECIFIED

(THERE WILL BE TWO INTERMISSIONS DURING THE COURSE OF THE PLAY)

Representing Mr. Williams	Liebling - Wood
Assistant to Lemuel Ayers on Scenery	Robert O'Hearn
Assistant to Lemuel Ayers on Costumes	Frank Thompson

Two lines quoted in Act III are from Four Quartets by T. S. Eliot. Copyright, 1936, by Harcourt Brace and Company, and used by permission of the publishers.

STAFF FOR "CAMINO REAL"

Company Manager	Robert C. Schnitzer	Orchestra Manager	Sol Gusikoff
Press Representative	Ben Washer	Musical Director	Betty Walberg
Consultant	Wolfe Kaufman	Master Carpenter	Louis Thomas
Production Stage Manager	Seymour Milbert	Master Electrician	Ralph Willis
Stage Manager	Thomajan	Assistant Electricians	Charles Garlinger
Production Assistant	Hope Abelson		Jack Carpenter
Production Secretary	Jeanette Kamins		Bruce Brewster
Legal Representative	H. William Fitelson	Master of Properties	Boyd C. Moorehead
Comptroller	Jean Fausel	Wardrobe Mistress	Isabel Duncan

CREDITS

Setting built and painted by Imperial Scenic Studios. Electrical equipment by Century Lighting Inc. Costumes executed by Eaves Costume Co. Sound by Masque Sound Engineering Co. Luggage by Amelia Earhart. Fabrics by Gladstone and Dozians. Stockings by Jessie Zimmer. Mr. Silvera's and Mr. Hatfield's shoes by LaRoy Boot Shop. Hair styles and hair pieces designed by Ronald De Mann, executed by Fleischer. Furniture by Newell Art Galleries. Dummies by Hecht. Suntan makeup by Helena Rubinstein. Julius Wile & Son Co. products used.

The Deodorizing Air Purifiers and the Creco Liquid Soap Dispensing System used in this theatre are manufactured by the Creco Company.

The Management is not responsible for personal apparel or property of patrons unless properly checked with the theatre attendant. Patrons are advised to take their coats and wraps with them whenever they leave their seats.

Ladies are requested to remove their hats.

Eli Wallach (Kilroy) and Joseph Anthony (Casanova) in the original New York production of *Camino Real*. Kilroy, the last of the wanderers, the ubiquitous soldier of fortune, the all-American kid, with a heart as big as a baby's head, wanders into the plaza of the Camino Real, becomes a patsy, and is nearly conned into despairing subjection like the other romantics trapped there.

The fiesta scene in *Camino Real* from which the confetti was cut as an economy measure when the play began to falter at the box office. Williams thinks it was the first time that the actors in a play left the stage and ran down into the audience. He felt that the play was flawed, but he also felt that it surpassed those flaws.

New Play

Camino Real (Cheryl Crawford, Ethel Reiner, Walter P. Chrysler Jr.). It is reasonable to suppose that Tennessee Williams thought that he had something to say in his latest play, and that he thought he was saying it. It isn't possible that he was deliberately playing an elaborate, depressing joke under a cloak of murky symbolism. Judging from the out-of-town reports, and from a limited reaction on opening night at New York's National Theater, there are people who know precisely what the playwright had in mind. But for the theatergoer of only normal intelligence and tolerance, the end result is a grand slam of bafflement and boredom, and a defeating sense of watching something that should be happening and never does.

Whatever his theatrical vagaries as a dramatist, Williams has proved that he is one of the modern American theater's best with "The Glass Menagerie," "A Streetcar Named Desire," and "The Rose Tattoo." If it is possible to describe his new play, it is a pretentious and misbegotten mixture of realism and fantasy, of masque and morbid morality. The Camino Real of the title is a weird and walled-in square in an unidentified tropic town to which only desperate people are admitted and from which very few escape. This much is clear. So is the fact that this sordid never-never land is peopled with mendicants, policemen disguised as Storm Troopers, and morticians disguised as street cleaners; with society's riffraff, rich and poor; and with Casanova, Camille, Lord Byron, Don Quixote, and, to clinch the whimsy, an ex-GI named Kilroy.

It is also clear that Tennessee Williams, usually sorry for Southern belles, is now very sorry for all humanity. Kilroy, the central figure, is a likable American prizefighter with a bad heart, and a natural patsy in the hands of Camino Real's evil overlord. As played by Eli Wallach, Kilroy is an appealing fall guy whose best escape from disillusion is death. Jo Van Fleet is a beautiful and disturbing Camille to play lover to Joseph Anthony's fading Casanova. Hurd Hatfield holds the stage eloquently as a remorseful Lord Byron. There are a number of other effective performances—Frank Silvera as the Mephisto of this limbo, Jennie Goldstein as a gypsy harridan, and particularly Barbara Baxley as her marketable daughter who (a new trick in mythology) is able to regain her virginity with each new moon.

There is no doubting the theatrical efficacy of some of Williams's scenes—Byron's lament for Shelley, the gypsy's blatant radio broadcast of her wares, the contrasting love scenes between Casanova and Camille, and between a fumbling Kilroy and the gypsy's wide-eyed (and postlunar) daughter. Sometimes the writing makes one remember that Williams can write both poetry and sharp, discerning dialogue. But the fact remains that no matter how many interpretations it is possible to give his pretentious exercise in flamboyance, not one of them seems to be worth the trouble. Elia Kazan has directed as if he thought otherwise, and comes to the rescue with an occasional broadside of physical and pictorial excitement.

Jo Van Fleet, as Camille, sheds a little light in Williams's dark world

Newsweek, March 30, 1953

Williams considers this review typical of the criticism he received for attempting new and different things in the theatre.

CONCERNING 'CAMINO REAL'

To the Drama Editor:

HAVING been in a play, in which it took quite a bit of time for the beauty and poetry to shine through, the now well recognized and honored "Come Back, Little Sheba," I am hoping that before the beautiful play of Tennessee Williams, "Camino Real," dies of malnutrition, people will realize what a treat it provides.

To me, it was stimulating, provocative, exciting, but certainly not mystifying.

I wish everyone could share this sense of exaltation.

SHIRLEY BOOTH.
New York.

"Posturing"

To the Drama Editor:

Your critic hails Tennessee Williams as "a gifted dramatist" and "a sincere writer" for his play, "Camino Real." The fact of the matter, as I see it, is that your critic has mistaken a melodramatic treatment of sensational deviations for the real thing. He has been taken in by a distressful kind of posturing and rhetoric with sentimentalized vacuity that he reveres as "poetry."

JOSEPH P. GREBANIER.
New York.

"Most Extraordinary"

To the Drama Editor:

May a visiting Englishwoman say how profoundly impressed and moved she was by "Camino Real."

I have long thought Mr. Williams a playwright of very great importance. I now believe him to be a very great playwright. I understand that various persons whose spiritual fare is "Chu-Chin-Chow" are conspiring to deprive us of this very great play. We have never sought to deprive them of the nonsense they like. Why are people who can see a little deeper to be deprived of a work which throws a blinding light on the whole of our civilization?

Verbally, intellectually, and visually (the décor is amazing) it is a most extraordinary work.

EDITH SITWELL.
New York.

"Childish Protest"

To the Drama Editor:

"Camino Real" is a childish protest against reality. A more mature writer would recognize the fact that millions of people understand the tragic horror of reality and that they stand humble before the facts.

This very humility is what saves them from utter despair, and gives the human race some slight semblance of dignity. Christ, far more aware than Tennessee Williams of the hideous and offensive aspects of life, showed us the only way. Our only hope of conquest is to stand humbly before the truth and to accept it without protest, living

New Play by Williams Is Lauded and Lambasted

out in our own lives that which we wish the human race could be.
Mrs. JEAN W. UNDERHILL.
Newark, N. J.

"Profoundly Stimulating"

To the Drama Editor:

I find myself baffled and shocked by the reviews which greeted Tennessee Williams' "Camino Real." Here is a superb production of a profoundly stimulating play which dares to try new methods and find new paths to the mind and heart.

Let us be humbly grateful to

The New York Times
Tennessee Williams.

Mr. Williams and his producers for their courage. And let our critics not dismiss so easily an exciting work which is one of the memorable experiences of many years of theatre-going and which may come to be a landmark.

WHITFIELD COOK.
Lyme, Conn.

Not Puzzled

To the Drama Editor:

Tennessee Williams, in his preliminary defense of "Camino Real," was "at a loss" to explain the precipitate exits of some members of the play's New Haven audience. He infers that these malcontents, unwilling to meet the play half way, had found it obscure and confusing.

As members of that same audience who were prevented from leaving by a kind of perverse fascination, may we suggest that some of the malcontents may have been impelled by the opposite reasons. The play, at least in its New Haven version, was crude and simple-minded.

Mr. Williams' much-vaunted "freedom" of form and expression does not seem to include freedom from clichés and tired symbolism. The play seems to be a random assemblage of properties left over

from, among others, Eliot, Saroyan, Steinbeck, Wilder, Cabell, and particularly Williams. Mr. Williams seems also to have profited from a poor college course in romanticism.

M. CHERNIAVSKY,
N. RUDICH,
E. C. MORRIS,
CHARLES MUSCATINE,
R. K. WEBB.
Middletown, Conn.

Great American Play

To the Drama Editor:

Certainly, "Camino Real" clarifies the author's stand as a playwright. To one playgoer (and obviously to a cheering and wildly appreciative audience) this excursion into the world of the unhappy relationship between man and fellow-man is unqualifiedly the great American play—for here, with bold, broad and sweeping strokes of his technicolor pen, Mr. Williams has created before us a panorama that we may not like to see, for it is all of us up there on the stage, and the public is not yet ready for truths about itself.

MARVIN GELBFISH.
New York.

One Who Left

To the Drama Editor:

In discussing "Camino Real," Mr. Williams made several comments regarding the people who left the theatre before the end of the performance. Since I am one of these people, I should like to state that I was not confused by the play and that I feel quite sure that my action was not the result of a threat to my security.

Has not Mr. Williams ignored one of the simplest reasons for leaving a play before its end? I just found the play dull and uninteresting.

H. G. FULLER.
New Britain, Conn.

Note of Sympathy

To the Drama Editor:

My sympathies to the four New York critics who almost dissuaded me from the most rewarding theatrical experience of the current season. That they could fail to find in "Camino Real" at least some of its lyric beauty, some of its throbbing emotion, some of its courageous power, is well nigh unbelievable.

To state that the play's pattern is confusing is to call life itself confusing. To state that the play's symbolism is ponderous and obscured from the audience is to ignore the audience's ardent, enthusiastic ovation at the final curtain.

The evening I visited the National, the patrons seemed to be reveling in a symbolism of their own: excitedly pounding palms together. Perhaps they sensed that, thanks to Tennessee Williams, the art of the drama had taken a step forward.

ARTHUR BROOKS.
New York.

On the beach at Ostia, near Rome, Williams had time to reflect on the upcoming film of *The Rose Tattoo*. It would introduce Anna Magnani to American audiences.

Williams met Anna Magnani in Rome during the summer of 1950. With Frank Merlo, who spoke Italian, breaking the way, the shyness and reserve with which Williams meets strangers soon evaporated, and he and Anna became fast friends. He admired her honesty and her beauty. "I never saw a more beautiful woman, enormous eyes, skin the color of Devonshire cream." Above all, he admired her ability to lead such an unconventional life, yet remain within touch of conventional society. She often said she preferred animals to people.

Anna Magnani's sketch of
Williams' dog Buffo.

*COLLECTION OF TENNESSEE
WILLIAMS*

Williams has had an array of pets that included, at one time or another, a cat named Gentleman Caller, a parrot named Laurita, an iguana of uncertain sex named Mr. Ava Gardner, a monkey named Creature, and a succession of English bulldogs named Mr. Moon, Buffo, Baby Doll, Miss Brinda, and Madame Sophia. He has also had a Belgian Shepherd named Satan and a Boston bull named Gigi. But his favorite of all was Miss Brinda, who had every possible defect including walleyes and practically no legs. She used to pose with the fashion models in Rome at the foot of the Spanish Steps, but never for any longer than one hour at a time.

COLLECTION OF TENNESSEE WILLIAMS

In Key West during the filming of *The Rose Tattoo,* Williams, Burt Lancaster, Anna, and Frank Merlo stand outside Williams' house, which served as a dressing room during the filming. Earlier, the film crew found a vacant lot and inquired about renting it for the goat chase. "I don't see why not," someone told them. "It belongs to Tennessee Williams." Both Williams and Merlo appeared in the film as customers in the bar scene.

DON PINDER, KEY WEST

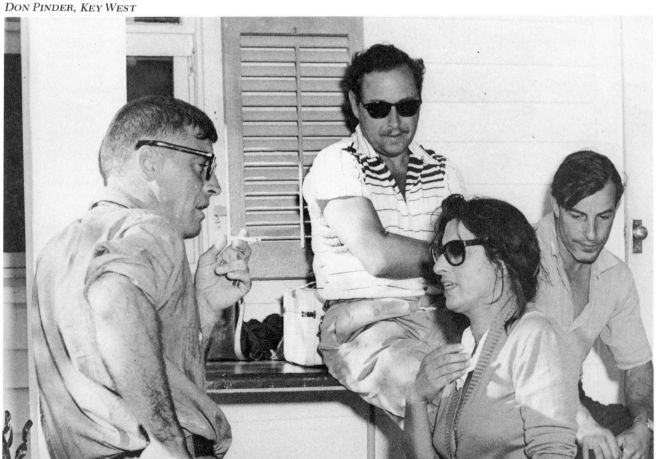

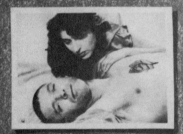

105

Anna Magnani won the Oscar for best actress in *The Rose Tattoo* in 1956, and the film was nominated in practically every category except Best Filmplay. An annoyed Williams wrote Audrey Wood that it was something he didn't want repeated. He felt that craven submission to censorship, a deep-rooted fear of risking offbeat distinction, playing it dully safe, had turned a very hastily written but original and moving script into the closest approximation of a regular Hollywood property raised above its level by one artist who simply couldn't be reduced to it.

Williams saw the filmed version of *The Rose Tattoo* in Key West with Gore Vidal and Maria Britneva. Through the years, beginning in Italy, Vidal and Williams have addressed each other as "Glorious Bird"—a reference from a poem by Shelley. Vidal still uses it, shortened now to "Bird." He and Williams complement each other, as friends should. Vidal is direct; Williams oblique. Maria Britneva, the Lady St. Just, and one of Williams closest friends, once observed that Truman Capote's voice was so high only a dog could hear it.

DON PINDER, KEY WEST

present

BARBARA BEL GEDDES
BURL IVES

in

The ELIA KAZAN Production

of

"CAT ON A HOT TIN ROOF"

A New Play

by

TENNESSEE WILLIAMS

with

Mildred Dunnock

and

Ben Gazzara

Scenery and Lighting by	Costumes by
JO MIELZINER	LUCINDA BALLARD

"And you, my father, there on the sad height,
Curse, bless me now with your fierce tears I pray.
Do not go gentle into that good night!
Rage, rage against the dying of the light!"
—DYLAN THOMAS

CAST
(In order of appearance)

MARGARET	BARBARA BEL GEDDES
BRICK	BEN GAZZARA
MAE, sometimes called Sister Woman	MADELEINE SHERWOOD
GOOPER, sometimes called Brother Man	PAT HINGLE
BIG MAMA	MILDRED DUNNOCK
DIXIE	PAULINE HAHN
BUSTER	DARRYL RICHARD
SONNY	SETH EDWARDS
TRIXIE	JANICE DUNN
BIG DADDY	BURL IVES
REVEREND TOOKER	FRED STEWART
DOCTOR BAUGH	R. G. ARMSTRONG
SOOKEY	MUSA WILLIAMS
DAISY	EVA VAUGHAN SMITH
LACEY	MAXWELL GLANVILLE
BRIGHTIE	BROWNIE McGEE
SMALL	SONNY TERRY

SCENE
The bed-sitting room of a plantation home in the Mississippi Delta.
An evening in summer. The action is continuous, with two intermissions.

Big Daddy (Burl Ives) and Maggie (Barbara Bell Geddes) are two of the most complete characters Williams has ever created. Maggie, the All-American girl with vitality, common sense and charm, is Big Daddy's favorite. He is the play's hero, a big man of violent emotions and a lust for money, food, love, and integrity. Like Williams' own father on whom he is modeled, Big Daddy has little rapport with his son, but he loves him and that's why he hurts him. Big Daddy's kingly magnitude makes him a favorite Williams character.

Young married couple took Junior out to th'zoo one Sunday, inspected all of God's creatures in their cages, with satisfaction. This afternoon was a warm afternoon in spring, an' that ole elephant had something else on his mind which was bigger'n peanuts. . . . Y'see, in the' cage adjoinin' was a young female elephant in heat! . . . That female elephant in the next cage was permeatin' the atmosphere about her with a powerful and excitin' odor of female fertility! . . . So this ole bull elephant still had a couple of fornications left in him. He reared back his trunk and got a whiff of that elephant lady next door!—began to paw at the dirt in his cage an' butt his head against the separatin' partition, and first thing y'know, there was a conspicious change in his *profile*—very *conspicious*! . . . So the little boy pointed at it and said, "What's that?" His Mam said, "Oh, that's—nothing!"—his Papa said, "She's spoiled!"

Big Mama (Mildred Dunnock) and Brick (Ben Gazzara) in *Cat on a Hot Tin Roof.* Critics found too much mystery in Brick's relationship with his dead friend Skipper and accused Williams of not answering a question after he'd raised it. Williams defended the characterization by saying that there should be mystery in character just as there is mystery in life.

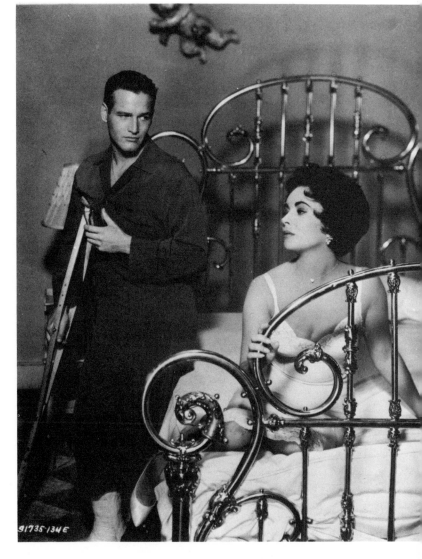

The double bed was fast becoming a Williams trademark. Williams considers Paul Newman second only to Brando as an actor. In typical Academy Award fashion, Elizabeth Taylor earned the award for *Cat on a Hot Tin Roof* but won it for *Butterfield 8.*

Liela Von Saher, "The Last of the Crepe de Chine Gypsies," Jane Bowles, and Williams aboard the SS *Queen Frederika.* Williams admires the late Jane Bowles above all other American writers of this century. He considers her play *In the Summer House* as standing quite above any other American play, an opinion shared by Harold Pinter. His gazebo in Key West is named The Jane Bowles Summer House.

Liela Von Saher was an amusing, tactless woman who once lured him to Stockholm and, in the opinion of Audrey Wood, severely hurt his chances for the Nobel Prize. The incident gives Gore Vidal one of his deadliest Williams' impressions.

COLLECTION OF TENNESSEE
WILLIAMS

Audrey Wood represented Tennessee for nearly 32 years. She personifies the meaning of "Lady" and "Professional." They are shown together at Marion Vaccaro's home in Miami during the Coconut Grove Playhouse run of either *Streetcar* or *Orpheus Descending* in the mid 1950's.

COURTESY OF AUDREY WOOD

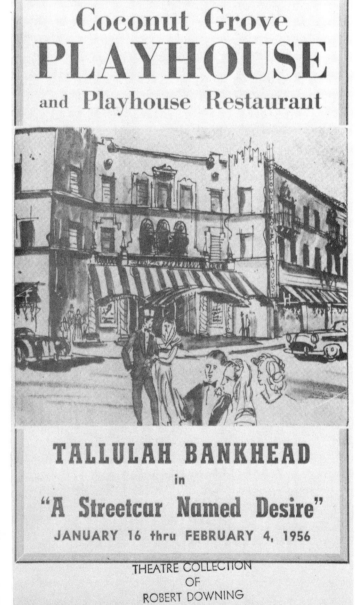

Coconut Grove
PLAYHOUSE
and Playhouse Restaurant

TALLULAH BANKHEAD
in
"A Streetcar Named Desire"
JANUARY 16 thru FEBRUARY 4, 1956

THEATRE COLLECTION
OF
ROBERT DOWNING

Tallulah Bankhead completely submerged herself in Blanche in the City Center production of *Streetcar*. Weeks earlier, in what Williams termed "her assault upon the role of Blanche" at Miami's Coconut Grove Playhouse, her performance had been more Bankhead than Blanche. Slightly in his cups after the show, he had muttered to a friend "that goddamn woman pissed on my play," a remark unfortunately picked up by *Time* magazine. Williams apologized profusely in the New York *Times*, and Bankhead noted that in so doing "Mr. Williams gives a lie to the ancient adage 'in vino veritas.'" Opening night in New York he knelt at her feet. She received his homage with queenly dignity, "as was her right," he said. He considered her the strongest of all the hurt people he's ever known.

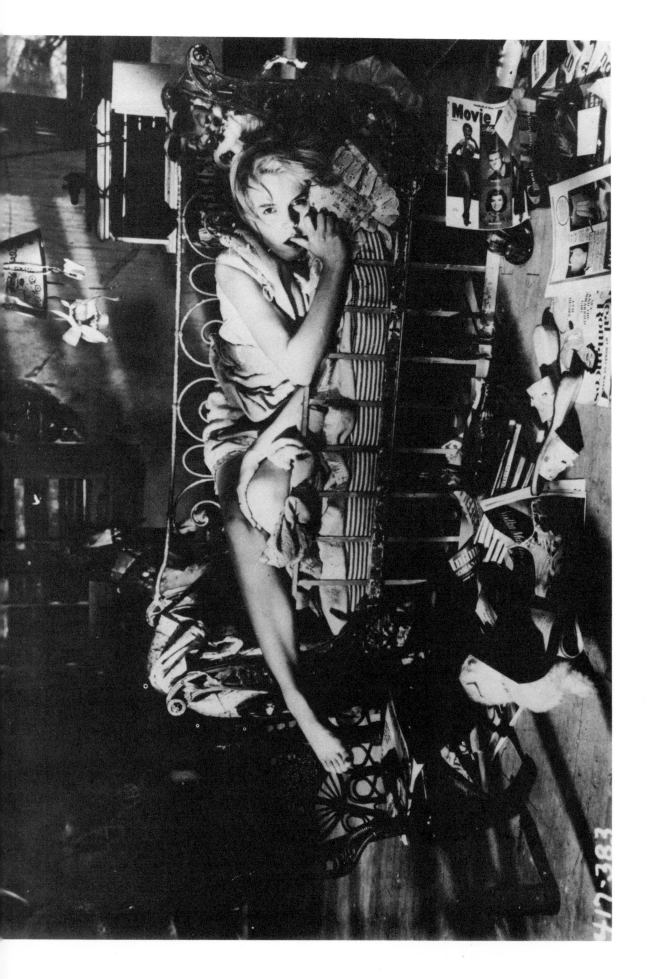

The notorious still from *Baby Doll* which was reproduced half a city block long near Duffy Square in New York. Williams first noticed the sign as he waited to cross 46th Street one summer night and was appalled by the size of his name. What he didn't notice directly across the street: his name also on the marquees of both the Palace and Loews State theaters. Three productions on Broadway!

Cardinal Spellman Denounces 'Baby Doll'

By Associated Press

NEW YORK, Dec. 16—Francis Cardinal Spellman, making one of his rare appearances in the pulpit of St. Patrick's Cathedral, today denounced the Warner Bros. film "Baby Doll" as "an immoral and corrupting influence."

The Roman Catholic Legion of Decency on Nov. 27 gave the picture a "C" or "condemned" rating and accused the Motion Picture Association of "open disregard" of its own code in approving the picture.

Elia Kazan, producer and director of the picture, and playwright Tennessee Williams, who wrote the story, issued statements in reply to Cardinal Spellman. Kazan said they had "tried to see" with "honesty and charity" the characters in the story.

Cardinal Spellman, the Archbishop of New York, said:

"The picture has been responsibly judged to be evil in concept and . . . is certain to exert an immoral and corrupting influence upon those who see it. . . .

"It is the moral and pa-

CARDINAL SPELLMAN

ELIA KAZAN

TENNESSEE WILLIAMS

triotic duty of every loyal citizen to defend America not only from dangers which threaten our beloved country from beyond our boundaries, but also the dangers which confront us at home.

"The conscienceless, venal attitude of the sponsors of this picture constitutes a definite corruptive moral influence. Since these degrading pictures stimulate immorality and crime they must be condemned and, therefore, . . . in solicitude for the welfare of my country, I exhort Catholic people from patroniz-

ing this film under pain of sin. . . ."

Kazan said in New York:

"I disagree that 'Baby Doll' is immoral. I am outraged by the charge that it is unpatri-

Continued on Page 11A.

Williams never could understand Cardinal Spellman's abuse of a film he'd never seen. He always thought *Baby Doll* was very innocent and very funny.

Cardinal Denounces Film 'Baby Doll'

Continued from Page 1A.

otic, and I fail to understand this.

"It is a personal story of four small pitiable people. Tennessee Williams and I have tried to see them with honesty and charity.

" 'Baby Doll' has been approved by the Motion Picture Authority of America, which is administered by men of discretion and conscience. It has been passed by the New York State Board of Censors.

"Cardinal Spellman or whoever saw the picture for him disagrees. But in this country judgments on matters of thought and taste are not handed down iron-clad from an unchallengeable authority. People see for themselves and finally judge for themselves,

and that's as it should be. It's our tradition and our practice. In the court of public opinion I'll take my chances."

Williams, in Key West, Fla., said in a statement issued in New York:

"I cannot believe that an ancient and august branch of the Christian faith is not larger in heart and mind than those who set themselves up as censors of a medium of expression that reaches all sections and parts of our country and extends the world over."

"Baby Doll" has a southern setting and involves a jealous cotton gin owner, his child bride and a young man she befriends. The picture will have its world premiere here next Tuesday.

Advertisements for the movie call it "Tennessee Williams' Boldest Story!" The picture stars Karl Malden, Eli Wallach and newcomer Carroll Baker.

Studio M Playhouse

Bird Road at Ponce de Leon Blvd., Coral Gables, Fla.

In Association with J. H. Keathley

Presents

Sweet Bird of Youth

by

TENNESSEE WILLIAMS

Directed, Lighting and Setting by GEORGE KEATHLEY

CAST

(In Order of Appearance)

Phil Beam	*Alan Mixon*	Edna	*Peggy Robinson*
Fly	*Gordon Albury*	Violet	*Fran Johnson*
George Scudder	*Paul Nagel, Jr.*	Bud	*Pat O'Neil*
Princess Pazmezoglu	*Margrit Wyler*	Scotty	*C. S. Hartley*
Valerie Finley	*Ruth Martin*	Stuff	*Hartley Joseph*
Nurse	*Fran Johnson*	Girl At Bar	*Ginger Riker*
Boss Finley	*James Reese*	Man At Bar	*Sheldon Frome*
Aunt Nonnie	*Blanche Kelly*	Miss Lucy	*Eleanor Sherman*
Fred Finley	*Robert Choromokos*		

SYNOPSIS OF SCENES

PART I

Scene 1. A suite in the Hotel Belvedere.
Scene 2. The same—a few minutes later.
Scene 3. The same—a short while later.

PART II

Scene 1. A Roman Catholic Church
Scene 2. The Clinic of Thomas J. Finley Hospital.
Scene 3. Breakfast room of Boss Finley's house
Scene 4. The bar of the Hotel Belvedere.
Scene 5. The porch of Boss Finley's house.
Scene 6. A speaker's platform.
Scene 7. The suite of the Hotel Belvedere.
Scene 8. The porch.

The entire action of the play takes place in the southern town of St. Cloud.
Time: The present.

There Will Be A Short Intermission After Part I

Author's Note

The stages in the making of a play are long and devious, as a rule, but on this occasion they have been short-cut much more than a little. By grace of unusual circumstances at least a year's work has been condensed into the space of a few weeks.

What you are seeing tonight is the production of the first draft of a play, something that ordinarily I would only dare to show to my literary agent, and even then with grave trepidations: it is a work in progress. If it is now in a state that's fit to be exposed to the public, that fact is creditable to the stimulating faith and daring, to the quick imagination and insight, of its director and to his players' gifts, including their patience. All the while this work has been in rehearsal, it has also been undergoing continual changes in dialogue and structure, even in basic theme and interpretation of character. At times Studio M has looked more like a printing press than a theatre, with stacks of re-writes, newly mimeographed, covering the stage and actors looking like a group of dazed proof-readers. I doubt that they will get the script out of their hands more than a day or two before dress-rehearsals. All of this has been very hard on them: it has been more than one adventure, not just one adventure.

This description of unique circumstances is *not* an attempt to disarm criticism. You will naturally judge this play as a completed work, and give it no special indulgence because it has been described to you as a work in progress.

At the same time, you may feel a sense of collaboration with us in the first making of something which is still being made.

Gratefully,

TENNESSEE WILLIAMS

Miami, April, 1956

Williams' production notes for *Sweet Bird of Youth*

Director/critic Harold Clurman, Williams, and Maureen Stapleton at the beginning of rehearsals for *Orpheus Descending.* Williams would find the New York production overwritten and underdirected. Harold Clurman was a big Williams booster.

JOSEPH ABELES STUDIO

JABE
BUZZARDS! BUZZARDS!
Maureen Stapleton (lady), Cliff Robertson (Val), and Crahan Denton (Jabe) in the original New York production of *Orpheus Descending.*

JOSEPH ABELES STUDIO

Lois Smith as Carol, and John Marriott as Uncle Pleasant the Conjure man in *Orpheus Descending.* Williams was sitting poolside in Miami with screenwriter Meade Roberts when a thorny problem arose concerning the gold ring Carol uses to purchase the snakeskin jacket in the filmed version, *The Fugitive Kind.* Williams stood, hitched up his swim shorts, and said, "He's going to get that gold ring if I have to appear in the goddamn film and *hand* it to him."

JOSEPH ABELES STUDIO

Martin Beck Theatre

Operated by Martin Beck Theatre Corp.

302 West Forty-fifth Street

Louis A. Lotito, Managing Director

FIRE NOTICE: The exit indicated by a red light and sign nearest to the seat you occupy is the shortest route to the street. In the event of fire please do not run—WALK TO THAT EXIT.
EDW. F. CAVANAGH, JR.
FIRE COMMISSIONER

Thoughtless persons annoy patrons and distract actors and endanger the safety of others by lighting matches during the performance and intermissions. This violates a city ordinance and renders the offender liable to ARREST. It is urged that all patrons refrain from lighting matches in the auditorium of this theatre.

THE · PLAYBILL · A · WEEKLY · PUBLICATION · OF · PLAYBILL · INCORPORATED

Beginning Thursday Evening, March 21, 1957

Matinees Wednesday and Saturday

OPENING NIGHT, MARCH 21, 1957

THE PRODUCERS THEATRE

presents

ORPHEUS DESCENDING

A New Play

by TENNESSEE WILLIAMS

STARRING

MAUREEN STAPLETON
CLIFF ROBERTSON

with

LOIS SMITH

JOANNA ROOS   CRAHAN DENTON   JANE ROSE
ELIZABETH EUSTIS   ROBERT WEBBER

Directed by HAROLD CLURMAN

Production Designed by BORIS ARONSON   Costumes by LUCINDA BALLARD

Lighting by FEDER

Produced by ROBERT WHITEHEAD

"I, too, am beginning to feel an immense need to become a savage and create a new world."
—August Strindberg in a letter to Paul Gauguin.

NEW YORK POST, FRIDAY, MARCH 22, 1957 60

TWO·on·the·AISLE

By Richard Watts Jr.

The World of Tennessee Williams

'Orpheus Descending'

A play by Tennessee Williams was presented last night at the Martin Beck Theater by the Producers' Theater. It was staged by Harold Clurman, and the set was by Boris Aronson. The cast included Maureen Stapleton, Cliff Robertson, Lois Smith, Joanna Roos, Crahan Denton, Jane Rose, Elizabeth Eustis, Robert Webber, Nell Harrison, Mary Farrell, John Marriott, R. G. Armstrong and Virgilia Chew.

"Orpheus Descending," which opened last night at the Martin Beck Theater, is another searing look at the dark and tormented world of Tennessee Williams. In the characteristic mood of its author, it is steeped in passion, hatred, frustration, bitterness and violence, and it ends in a welter of blood and death worthy of one of the Elizabethan tragedies. It abounds in tension, blackness of spirit, and the deep sadness of misunderstood loneliness. And, splendidly acted and staged, it is a drama of notable power, grim poetic insight and disturbing fascination.

More than most of Mr. Williams' plays, it contemplates not only the personal tragedies of a few frustrated misfits, but also the ugly tensions, hatreds, jealousies and narrow-minded stupidities of an entire backwoods Southern community. There are loathsome people in it who could well serve as melodramatic villains, but the actual villain is the petty and spiteful atmosphere of this small unnamed town, and the air of doom that hangs over the drama is an almost impersonal kind of vindictiveness which the playwright sets down with bitter understanding.

Central Figures

The people in whom "Orpheus Descending" is centrally interested, though, are the lost and embittered daughter of an Italian immigrant, a woman tormented by the knowledge that some of the customers who come to her store had been in the masked mob that had murdered her father, and a wild and imaginative young vagrant, who is looking for an unaccustomed peace and quiet and finds only destruction. It is their dual tragedy that provides the narrative, and their doom comes in an outburst of violence which provides one of the author's most harrowing endings.

They are not, however, the only characters studied with the sort of gloomy compassion which Mr. Williams presents in his capacity as brooding dramatic poet of evil. There is, for one, the girl prostitute of "good" family, whose preoccupation with sex is the tortured reaction from one-time social idealism. For another, there is the half-crazed wife of the sheriff, who is looking for release from memories of her husband's sadistic official activities. As an expert in pity and terror, the playwright makes both of them memorable figures.

Power and Passion

Possibly because it is concerned with the depiction of an entire community, "Orpheus Descending" seems a little more scattered in its drama than is usually the case with Mr. Williams. That ending in blood and death is perhaps a bit too precipitous to be completely effective. But the power, the passion and the violent credibility are there, and so is that remarkable gift for being darkly lyric in the midst of terror and hatred. There are occasions, too, when a wry and embittered humor emerges with unexpected force in the center of the unrelieved gloom.

Harold Clurman's staging and Boris Aronson's set capture the play's mood admirably. And the performances are brilliant. Maureen Stapleton again proves what a splendid actress she is as the doomed woman, and Cliff Robertson seems just right as the young, music-loving vagrant. Lois Smith is deeply moving as the young prostitute, while Joanna Roos as the sheriff's wife, and Crahan Denton, as the heroine's dying but still homicidal husband, are particularly effective. The black and brooding spirit of Tennessee Williams is once more fascinatingly dramatized.

Williams met Jean-Paul Sartre and Simone de Beauvoir (center) in Havana during the first year of Castro's regime. Williams also met the Cuban leader through a letter of introduction from Ernest Hemingway and after first accepting an invitation to attend the afternoon's executions ("I think a writer should experience everything, don't you?"). He declined when Marion Vaccaro said, "Tommy, those are *people* he's shooting." Williams admired both Castro and Sartre; theologian Paul Tillich once referred a student of existentialism to the plays of Tennessee Williams.

COLLECTION OF TENNESSEE WILLIAMS

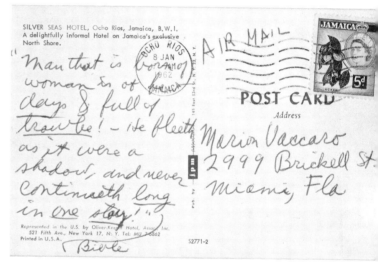

Williams' natural high good-humor is often evident in amusing cards. When he and Marion struck off together, the watchword was "Sister, March."

COURTESY OF GEORGE ROBISON BLACK

"Ballin' the jack" in Jamaica.
COURTESY OF GEORGE ROBISON BLACK

The Cornstalk House in New Orleans' Garden District is typical of the lovely homes in that section of the city. Williams used *Garden District* as an umbrella title for *Suddenly Last Summer* and *Something Unspoken* because of their common setting.

Williams met Nancy Venable aboard ship, and as he occasionally does, he used her name in a play. She became a dear friend he always thought of as "Eleanor of Aquitaine." She recorded parts of the character Margaurite Gautier from *Camino Real,* and was one of the few people most concerned about him in the dark days ahead. Sadly, she died in the prime of life.

Williams at an early rehearsal of *Suddenly Last Summer.* It was his friend Herbert Machiz's inspired casting that brought Anne Meacham into the play as Catherine Holly, with Robert Lansing, who played Dr. Sugar. Machiz would later direct Diana Barrymore to critical acclaim in a touring company. Williams is aware that *Suddenly Last Summer* contains some of his best writing.

York Playhouse

JOHN C. WILSON AND WARNER LE ROY

present

GARDEN DISTRICT

by TENNESSEE WILLIAMS

with

ANNE MEACHAM   **HORTENSE ALDEN**   **ELEANOR PHELPS**

ROBERT LANSING   NANON-KIAM   ALAN MIXON   DONNA CAMERON

Directed by HERBERT MACHIZ

Settings by ROBERT SOULE   Lighting by LEE WATSON
Costumes by STANLEY SIMMONS   Incidental music by NED ROREM

SOMETHING UNSPOKEN

Cast in Order of Appearance

Cornelia Scott ....ELEANOR PHELPS
Grace Lancaster ....HORTENSE ALDEN

Time: the present
A room in the Garden District of New Orleans
Intermission

SUDDENLY LAST SUMMER

Mrs. Venable ....HORTENSE ALDEN
Dr. Cukrowicz ....ROBERT LANSING
Miss Foxhill ....DONNA CAMERON
Mrs. Holly .... ELEANOR PHELPS
George Holly .... ALAN MIXON
Catherine Holly ....ANNE MEACHAM
Sister Felicity .... NANON-KIAM

The Garden District of New Orleans
The early thirties: a late afternoon in spring

PROGRAM CREDITS

Miss Meacham's and Miss Alden's shoes by Andrew Geller. Pearls by Marvella. Gloves by Van Raalte. Handbags by Lewis Purses. Feathers by Hayflitch. Furs by Peterzill & Cohen. Fabrics courtesy Mollie Parnis and Leon Livingston. Fabrics by Gladstone. Miss Phelp's hat by Eve Shelly. Silver Service by Sarah and Simon Wimborne of London. Miss Alden's wig by Ira Senz. Sound equipment by Masque Sound. Sound recordings by Jerry Newman. Lighting system designed and executed by Roy Newman. Sewing machine by Mrs. Marcus Jaffe. Costumes dry-cleaned by Ernest Winzer Inc. Costumes executed by Barbara Spence.

Diana Barrymore as Catherine Holly scored a great personal success in a touring production of *Suddenly Last Summer* with Cathleen Nesbitt as Mrs. Venable. Barrymore's great dream was to play *Sweet Bird of Youth* in London where it had never been produced. Williams listened to her read but felt that she was too much like the Princess and told her that her performance would hold no surprise. She never accepted his judgment, and her obsession with the play tormented her until her tragic death a short time later.

JOSEPH ABELES STUDIO

Williams personally sold the film rights of *Suddenly Last Summer* by telephone to Sam Spiegel. Gore Vidal wrote the script, and Williams figured that the movie was as bad as the profits were good.

Sebastian Venable in sacrificial white runs to his martyrdom in the white-hot blazing day in this cannibalistic metaphor that is a parable of the human condition.

Williams was a daily visitor on the set of *The Fugitive Kind*.

On the set of *The Fugitive Kind,* the filmed version of *Orpheus Descending,* Marlon Brando and Anna Magnani were wary competitors. Brando said that during his scenes with her he would carry a rock in each hand, but it was Anna Magnani who should have carried the rocks.

GOTHAM BOOK MART, COURTESY OF ANDREAS BROWN

123

Geraldine Page (The Princess Kosomopolis) played the legendary Ariadne in *Sweet Bird of Youth* to Paul Newman's Chance Wayne. She offers the sacred hero a route of escape from the labyrinth, but as Adonis, he chooses to remain and offer himself as a blood sacrifice. They are both monsters, but she has a will that he lacks. *JOSEPH ABELES STUDIO*

MARTIN BECK THEATRE

CHERYL CRAWFORD
presents

PAUL NEWMAN   GERALDINE PAGE

SIDNEY BLACKMER

in

SWEET BIRD OF YOUTH

Relentless caper for all those who step
The legend of their youth into the noon
—Hart Crane

A New Play by

TENNESSEE WILLIAMS

Directed by

ELIA KAZAN

with

RIP TORN	DIANA HYLAND	MADELEINE SHERWOOD	LOGAN RAMSEY

MARTINE BARTLETT   CHARLES TYNER

Settings and Lighting by
JO MIELZINER
Music by
PAUL BOWLES
Costumes by
ANNA HILL JOHNSTONE

125

Jane Fonda, whom Williams admires tremendously, starred in the filmed version of *Period of Adjustment*. He once proposed a toast to her mid-Atlantic en route to Italy during the height of America's Vietnam involvement, and to his amusement all the startled first-class guests responded. He prefers her politics to those of Bob Hope.

The Night of the Iguana would be Williams' longest, most appalling tour with any play, culminating in Chicago when he nearly died from a dog bite inflicted by his Belgian shepherd Satan, and where Bette Davis ordered director Frank Corsaro first out of the theater and then out of the city "back to that goddamn Actors Studio." Williams modeled Nonno, the world's oldest living poet, after his grandfather Dakin.

JOSEPH ABELES STUDIO

Williams Wins 3rd N.Y. Drama Prize

NEW YORK, April 10 (UPI) —Playwright Tennessee Williams won his third New York Drama Critics' Circle Award for the best American play of a Broadway season when "The Night of the Iguana" topped the annual voting today.

Robert Bolt's British drama, "A Man For All Seasons," won the citation as the best foreign play.

"How To Succeed In Business Without Really Trying," by Abe Burrows, Jack Weinstock and Willie Gilbert, with score by Frank Loesser, was cited as the best musical of the 1961-62 season.

"Iguana," at the Royale Theater, received 12 of the 18 votes cast. The other six went to Paddy Chayefsky's Biblical play, "G i d e o n," at the Plymouth Theater.

Bolt's drama, in which Paul Scofield is starring at the Anta Theater, received 15 votes and three went to Harold Pinter's "The Caretaker," which closed in February after 165 performances.

"How To Succeed," current at the 46th Street, got 17 of the 18 votes.

Williams previously had been honored by the Circle for "A Streetcar Named Desire" in 1948 and for "Cat On A Hot Tin Roof" in 1955.

Diana Barrymore entertained the notion of marrying Williams, something he considered one of her better jokes. She was generous and delightful, and he admired her sharp wit and her raucous sense of the ridiculous. He thought of her as an engine running out of control, laboring under the weight of a name too much to live up to. She was a delightful traveling companion and he roared when, after Marion Vaccaro made flight reservations in his name, they were met by the VIP Host at the airport and Barrymore turned to him and said, "You see what the Barrymore name means?"

Sadly, within ten years of the death of Diana Barrymore, Williams would lose two of his dearest friends in the passing of Jane Bowles and Marion Black Vaccaro.

For Diana Barrymore

Yellow, yellow roses, for the loves I have known...

Valley lillies for loves I never knew...

Violets to say farewell to all that might have been.

        Valley lillies tight in my fist
        Cold...holding dreams,
        dreams no longer warm or needed

I did wait for you, Godot...but you got here sooner.

So quiet and gently...like an old friend.

    without saying the name

        or announcing the visit.
            In my house there is always welcome

            For everyone.

Tommorrow

            When the flames and the hot fire take me,
                PLEASE PLEASE

            save the yellow roses
                violets I will hold.
            Keep the valley lillies...
            for the bright lighting exit into the unknown.

NOW

            Well, anyway, I am warm
            warm with remembered love and dreams.

Prehaps
I may never fly

        I may try
        if they rent me a set of wings.

    Never shall I be cold again...no, not ever

            For you and you and you and you,
            Here is a Heart of Violets
                in the center

            a Red red rose.

                        Goodnight...Goodnight.

                    Marion Black Vaccaro

Two

If there wasn't a thing in the world called Time, the passing of time in the world we live in, we might be able to count on things staying the same, but time lives in the world with us and has a big broom and is sweeping us out of the way, whether we like it or not. —*I Can't Imagine Tomorrow.*

WRIGHT LANGLEY, KEY WEST

PART 4

I Rise in Flame, Cried the Phoenix

4

I Rise in Flame, Cried the Phoenix

> Whoever you are—I have always depended on the kindness of strangers.
>
> —Blanche
> *A Streetcar Named Desire*

The critical success of *The Night of the Iguana* thrust Williams to a new pinnacle in his professional life. *Time* magazine's cover story hailed him as "the greatest living playwright in the English-speaking world," and indeed, his reputation was worldwide. In every major country his work was constantly performed. Awards and recognition continued to be showered on him. He held four New York Drama Critics' Awards and two Pulitzer Prizes. Hollywood had filmed thirteen major works. His professional earnings exceeded several million dollars. But during the early years of the decade of the sixties, his personal life tottered on the brink of a crisis which threatened to destroy him.

Since the summer of 1955 in Rome when he washed down Seconals with martinis, he had come more and more to depend on various drugs and stimulants to enable him first to work and then to sleep. For years he had been unable to start down a street unless he saw a bar in it, and although often it remained untouched, he liked a martini close at hand during his morning work. Usually just the presence of a drink was enough to reassure him and quell any panic he might feel.

When Frank Merlo developed incurable cancer, Williams' personal life began to deteriorate, and when Merlo died, the life he had created for Williams died with him. Without this to sustain him, Williams plunged into a depres-

sion which lasted for seven years. He would call it his stoned age.

He continued to write, of course—it was a fatal need—and his work continued to be produced, but the great years of critical acclaim and long Broadway runs appeared to be over. The descent began gradually with the respectable failure of *The Milk Train Doesn't Stop Here Anymore,* a dramatic statement about an aging woman dictating her memoirs on the Divina Costeria as the end of her life and death approaches. He developed the play from his excellent story, "Man Bring This Up Road," and *Milk Train* was first produced at the Festival of Two Worlds in Spoleto. Herbert Machiz directed the British actress Hermione Baddeley, and she was a brilliant Flora Goforth. Williams insisted on her for Roger Stevens' Broadway production, and her great personal notices more than justified his faith in her. Unfortunately, the play had the misfortune to open during the newspaper strike of 1963. The cool reception from the critics, together with the news blackout, doomed the play to a brief run. When David Merrick produced the second New York version, Williams cast Tallulah Bankhead as Flora Goforth, but it was already too late in her career. She had lost the necessary physical vigor which the role demanded, but out of deference to her, the play was allowed to limp into New York, where the critics demolished it.

Williams still likes the play and considers it a

great vehicle for the right actress. In spite of the obvious miscasting of the Burtons—Taylor was too young and Burton was too old—he also likes the film version, *Boom,* and thinks that one day it will be recognized as an artistic success.

Shortly after Frank Merlo's death in New York, Williams returned to Key West, where his behavior grew increasingly erratic. It culminated in his living completely alone, something he had never done before. Desperate for a solution to his depression, he returned to New Orleans and tried to pull himself together. He leased a charming two-story house on Dauphine Street—a house restored by the late Clay Shaw and one he would later purchase—and from there he journeyed back and forth to his New York apartment, where he continued to isolate himself from everyone, ignoring both the telephone and the doorbell. Through the intercession of his cousin Jim Adams, he moved to a different apartment in New York. Shortly thereafter he became the patient of a doctor he referred to as "The Witch Doctor" or "Dr. Feelgood," who gave him marvelous injections which freed him from depression and tension and permitted him to work with great ease and speed. "Speed" was the word. Soon he was carrying his own little vials and injecting himself every morning. It made the work possible, but he was also taking Doriden and Mellaril at the same time. The combination proved debilitating to the point where he had great difficulty keeping his balance and frequently fell down. The mornings were fine, but he led a zombielike existence throughout the rest of the day.

Under the influence of "speed," he wrote one of his favorite plays, and he never found writing so easy. *The Gnädiges Fräulein,* together with another short play called *The Mutilated,* was produced in New York under the collective title *Slapstick Tragedy.* Ruthless reviews closed the production in four days, something unheard of for a Williams play.

His last respectable failure on Broadway was the long play *Kingdom of Earth,* produced by David Merrick as *The Seven Descents of Myrtle.* It was a tragedy set in the Delta country, but like *The Rose Tattoo,* the play also had great flashes of Williams' humor. A preproduction movie deal helped curb the losses from a disappointingly short run on Broadway.

At home in Key West, weary, depressed, and extremely ill from the Hong Kong flu, Williams was visited by his younger brother, Dakin, an attorney from Collinsville, Illinois, who was concerned about his brother's health. Years earlier as a young Air Force officer in India, Dakin had converted to Roman Catholicism. Later, he coauthored a book defending the faith, and now in Key West he used his convert's zeal to instigate his brother's conversion as well.

Williams had been brought up as a High Church Episcopalian, and the rites and beliefs of the Roman Church were familiar to him. For years he had kept a small tacky statue of the Infant of Prague standing on a penny in his various apartments, and so one day after he received extreme unction from a Jesuit priest for his bout with the flu, he was baptized into the church as Francis Xavier in the presence of a few close friends and his maid of twenty-five years. He had never been a regular churchgoer, nor did he now become one. He later dismissed the idea by saying he figured the Lord would just as soon have him working as mumbling.

After a quick trip to Rome following his conversion, still weary and unwell, he returned to Key West and concluded arrangements for the Off-Broadway production of *In the Bar of A Tokyo Hotel.* It was symptomatic of his condition at this time that he recalls neither his visitors nor the details of the discussion. The play opened in New York, and despite the talent of Anne Meacham and Donald Madden, it represented a low point in his professional career. *Time* magazine observed that it was more worthy of a coroner's report than a review.

When the play folded, he fled New York with Anne Meacham and headed for Tokyo to catch a new production of *A Streetcar Named Desire.* They sailed from New York aboard the SS *President Cleveland* for Bangkok by way of Honolulu. It was there that he casually mentioned the word "cancer" to a journalist over mai tais. The press instantly reported that he was dying of the dread disease, and the ensuing publicity pursued a startled Williams across the Pacific to Yokohama to Hong Kong to Bangkok, where a Thai army surgeon who had studied in the States did perform a relatively minor operation under local anesthesia.

Shortly after he flew home to Key West from Tokyo, Marion Vaccaro visited him. Shocked and alarmed by his condition, she immediately alerted Audrey Wood, who in turn called his brother, Dakin. Williams remembers being at the Key West Airport and then in his mother's home in St. Louis, where they managed to talk him into entering Barnes Hospital. Once he was there, they signed a furious Williams into a confinement which lasted three months. He suffered convulsions, at least one coronary, and endless torment at being confined—something he had always dreaded throughout his life. But he resolved to survive, and like Mother Goddam, he survived it all. He was released just before Christmas in 1969. His anger at his mother and his brother has since cooled, but a great many harsh things were said at the time. He remains concerned about his mother—she is in her nineties now—and he speaks to his brother again, but he was a long time getting over the ordeal.

Something else from this dark period in his life was his final separation from Audrey Wood, his agent for nearly thirty-two years. He felt, rightly or wrongly, that she became detached from his increasingly desperate circumstances during the sixties, and following a brief scene backstage during the Chicago tryout of *Out Cry*, he dropped her. He remained with the same agency, now known as ICM (International Creative Management, Inc.), but he chose a young southerner named Bill Barnes to represent him. Barnes would become one of his closest personal friends.

Williams' phoenixlike recovery from the ashes of the preceding seven years began with a poetry reading in London, England. A successful Off-Broadway production of a new play, *Small Craft Warnings*, did much to hearten him, and he began a swift return to his old self. He worked on a novel about a dream he had concerning his early life in Greenwich Village, and he began to write his memoirs.

He developed *Small Craft Warnings* from a short work called *Confessional*. The play is a statement about a group of ordinary, sometimes defeated, and often courageous castoffs grappling with survival and existence in a Pacific coast bar. He was also preoccupied with getting a first-class production for his two-character play, now called *Out Cry*, and to this end, he began appearing in the play *Small Craft Warnings* as "Doc" during the summer doldrums. His appearances helped the box office, and to further stimulate the play's run, he began conducting symposia from the stage following the nightly performances, occasionally helped by such friends in the audience as Maureen Stapleton and Claire Luce.

He nearly reached his objective; *Small Craft Warnings* ran just a few weeks short of the six months he had hoped for, and *Out Cry* was produced on Broadway. The play is a cry of the heart—a plea for survival; a dramatic poem about a brother and a sister, both actors, stranded in a theater in a play-within-a-play in a nameless place. . . .He considered it a major work, and its instant failure on Broadway was a bitter personal disappointment to him. *Out Cry* was a play very close to his heart, and though his writing was much more personal now, he felt that the failure was really due to the difficulty of casting the right leads who would be strong enough to carry such a static play.

He finished the novel about his early life in the Village, *Moise and the World of Reason*, and the book is interesting primarily because in it Williams-the-writer tells about Williams-the-playwright, who appears as a character. The novel received mixed notices. Work on his memoirs continued, and what he termed "his last long play" (there have been three to date) opened in Boston for a six-week pre-Broadway run at the Shubert Theater. The play was scheduled to move on to Washington for a month and then go into New York.

The Red Devil Battery Sign is a tragic love story, but also symbolic of the decay in America during the last fifteen years. It is set in Dallas just after the Kennedy assassination, and it is Williams' first play with political overtones. The Boston tryout starred Claire Bloom, fresh from her London triumph as Blanche in a revival of *Streetcar*, and Anthony Quinn, who had been one of Williams' personal choices for Stanley in the original New York production of *Streetcar*.

Boston audiences were attentive and enthusiastic, and critic Elliot Norton found much to admire and like about the new work, but in the end, it seemed a case of too many producers, some miscasting, and the need for considerable rewriting. David Merrick closed the show in Boston, and with his dog Madame Sophia, Williams flew off to Rome, "devastated." *Time* magazine quoted Anthony Quinn, "I'd rather be in a flop by Tennessee Williams, whom I consider to be the world's greatest living playwright than in a hit by a shit."

In his battle for personal and artistic survival, Williams, like the Gnädiges Fräulein has never been completely defeated. His position as one of the greatest playwrights in the history of the

American theater has become like her tattered theatrical costume, made all the more brilliant as he wears his commercial failures like spangles of blood that glitter like rubies.

Work progressed on his memoirs, but Doubleday would publish just half the material he submitted. Critics commented on the explicitness with which he revealed his personal life, but they also commented on the total honesty with which he described it. It soon made the best-seller list and stayed there for several weeks.

His autograph party in Doubleday's 56th Street bookstore shattered all existing records, and frantic officials had to send out and borrow more books.

When Gore Vidal told Williams that he didn't miss a thing by sleeping through the decade of the sixties, he also said, "If you missed the sixties, Bird, God knows what you are going to do with the seventies."

As the decade of the 1970s began, *Small Craft Warnings, Moise and the World of Reason*, and his *Memoirs* were openers in the early years of a decade which would see as many as four Williams plays revived to critical acclaim in a single New York season.

In 1977, New Directions brought out his second book of poems, *Androgyne, Mon Amour.* Waiting in the wings is a completed screenplay based on his famous story *One Arm.* Also finished and awaiting the right time is *Stopped Rocking*, a teleplay written for Maureen Stapleton and inspired by an incident that occurred during his confinement in Barnes hospital. He is finishing another novel, and a new play, *Tiger Tail* (based on *Baby Doll*) is scheduled for a premiere production in Atlanta as this book goes to press.

Tennessee Williams, a vigorous sixty-seven in 1978, retains his famous drive and energy. He talks some of retiring to a small farm in Sicily where he would raise goats and ducks, but for a compulsive writer whose work is his life and who himself has said, "Plays do not exist until they are on the stage," who would bet a nickel that he won't be heard from again and again, perhaps in a very major way?

CARICATURE

FAMED CARICATURIST AL HIRSHFELD DEPICTS THE EXCITING CHARACTERS IN "THE NIGHT OF THE IGUANA"

America's most famous caricaturist, Al Hirshfeld, brings to life the principals of the Ray Stark-John Huston production of "The Night of the Iguana," screen version of Tennessee Williams' prize-winning Broadway play, presented by Metro-Goldwyn-Mayer and Seven Arts Productions. In the foreground are Richard Burton in his role as the defrocked minister, Rev. Lawrence Shannon, and Ava Gardner as Maxine, fiery proprietor of a hotel in Mexico. Slightly to the rear is Sue Lyon as Charlotte, the teen-ager who becomes infatuated with Burton. At left, Deborah Kerr and Cyril Delevanti, cast respectively as an artist and her poet grandfather, who also become involved in Burton's turbulent life. "The Night of the Iguana" was filmed entirely on locations in Mexico, largely in the colorful fishing village of Mismaloya on the Pacific coast. This art is available as a photo, and also in 3, 4, and 5 column mat sizes. Order by number from National Screen Service.

Still No. NOI-Pos 8 — 3-Column Mat-3X, 4-Column Mat-4X, 5-Column Mat-5X

Spurred on by Hedda Hopper, the world held its breath waiting for the fireworks from the highly charged *Night of the Iguana* cast. They were disappointed.

Williams was an attentive visitor on the *Iguana* set in Puerto Vallarta, Mexico. He was disappointed that John Huston's ending of the film wasn't more poetic.

COLLECTION OF TENNESSEE WILLIAMS

Williams quit smoking following Frank Merlo's death from lung cancer, and Marion Vaccaro set this picture up with his dog Gigi to encourage him.

COURTESY OF GEORGE ROBISON BLACK

DAVID MERRICK

presents

HARRY GUARDINO   **ESTELLE PARSONS**

BRIAN BEDFORD

in

THE SEVEN DESCENTS OF MYRTLE

A NEW PLAY BY

TENNESSEE WILLIAMS

Setting and Lighting by   Costumes by
JO MIELZINER   **JANE GREENWOOD**

Associate Producer
SAMUEL LIFF

Directed by

JOSÉ QUINTERO

OPENS WED. EVG. MAR. 27 • MAIL ORDERS NOW
PREVIEWS MON. and TUES. EVGS. MAR. 25 & 26

PRICES: All Evgs. Including Opening: Orch. $7.50; Front Mezz. $6.90; Rear Mezz. $5.75, 4.80, 3.60. Mats. Wed. and Sat.
Orch. $5.50; Front Mezz. $4.80; Rear Mezz. $4.05, 3.60, 3.00. Please enclose stamped, self-addressed envelope with mail
orders. Kindly specify several alternate dates. **OPENING NIGHT SEATS AVAILABLE.**

First Mat. Thurs. Mar. 28 at 2:30 P.M.
ETHEL BARRYMORE THEATRE, 243 W. 47th St., N.Y. 10036

PRIOR TO BROADWAY PHILADELPHIA—WALNUT ST. THEATRE—MAR. 18 thru 23

Williams' opening night ticket stub.

Playbill cover, *Seven Descents*

Originally titled *Kingdom of Earth,* David Merrick produced this tragicomedy of the Delta as *The Seven Descents of Myrtle,* symbolizing, one supposes, Dante's image of Hell as a seven-storey mountain. Estelle Parsons was brilliant in a role written for Maureen Stapleton. Williams prefers his original title.

PREMIERE PERFORMANCE JANUARY 16, 1963

MOROSCO THEATRE

ROGER L. STEVENS

presents

HERMIONE
BADDELEY

MILDRED
DUNNOCK

PAUL
ROEBLING

in

THE MILK TRAIN DOESN'T STOP HERE ANYMORE

A New Play by
TENNESSEE WILLIAMS

with

ANN WILLIAMS

CLYDE VENTURA

MARIA TUCCI

Settings and Lighting by
JO MIELZINER

Costume Supervision by
FRED VOELPEL

From Sketches by
PETER HALL

Music by
PAUL BOWLES

Associate Producers
LYN AUSTIN and **VICTOR SAMROCK**

Directed by
HERBERT MACHIZ

The original New York production of *The Milk Train Doesn't Stop Here Anymore* starred Hermione Baddeley as Flora Goforth, Mildred Dunnock as the Witch of Capri, and Paul Roebling as Christopher Flanders, the Angel of Death.

JOSEPH ABELES STUDIO

Hermione Baddeley as Flora Goforth in *Milk Train*. Anna Magnani, watching her performance at the Festival of Two Worlds in Spoleto, exclaimed, *"Com' è magnifico!"* In New York she received estatic personal notices. Williams admires her as a brilliant actress who is also very warm-hearted.

JOSEPH ABELES STUDIO

DAILY NEWS, THURSDAY, JANUARY 2, 1964

Miss Bankhead Lacks Steam in Second Run of 'The Milk Train'

By JOHN CHAPMAN

Tennessee Williams' "The Milk Train Doesn't Stop Here Anymore," which was reproduced at the Brooks Atkinson Theatre last evening by David Merrick, is a simplified and rather awkwardly stylized version of the drama which was presented about a year ago during the newspaper blackout.

In his effort to clarify the play, which still is rather mystical, Williams has, in my mind, lessened its emotional appeal. And Tallulah Bankhead's performance of the central character seems plaintive, whereas the original Flora Goforth, as portrayed by Hermione Baddeley, was heroic.

Heroic Old Bat

And a heroic Flora Goforth was whom Williams was writing about in both versions. This

Tab Hunter
Somewhat poetic

woman, whose life has entailed wild excess and success, will live only two more days, but she won't admit the approach of death because she is afraid to face it. When a rather mysterious young man, who seems to be a sculptor of mobiles and a one-volume poet, appears and seeks to help her toward the threshold, she will have none of his help.

Flora Goforth is a very wealthy old bat who once was a Follies girl. She has wed and buried several rich husbands. Now, in a villa overlooking the Mediter-

---

"THE MILK TRAIN DOESN'T STOP HERE ANYMORE"

Play by Tennessee Williams, produced by David Merrick at the Brooks Atkinson Theatre, Jan. 1, 1964.

THE CAST

Stage Assistants	Bobby Dean Hooks
	Konrad Matthaei
Mrs. Goforth	Tallulah Bankhead
Blackie	Marian Seldes
Rudy	Ralph Roberts
Christopher Flanders	Tab Hunter
Witch of Capri	Ruth Ford

---

ranean coast of Italy, she is dictating her memoirs to an overworked secretary.

In the original production, this villa was vast and luxurious and bugged with loudspeakers in every room, including the secretary's bedroom, so that Flora might dictate a memory day or night, whenever booze, pills or pain prompted her.

Stylized All Over

In the new production, designed by Rouben Ter-Arutunian, the stage is backed by a a mellow, golden cyclorama and in the middle of it is a rather Oriental box with sliding panels and a bed inside. Most of what action there is takes place in front of the panels, but when occasion arises two stylized "stage assistants" move the panels and offer a comment or two on what is going on.

The setting didn't stimulate my imagination much, and neither did Miss Bankhead. She could roar the old Bankhead roar once in a while and get loud laughter from one of the queerest audiences since the early days of the Ballet Russe de Monte Carlo. But she did not arouse in me the pity that Williams originally wrote into her part, and often she was unintelligible.

Tab Hunter does a pretty good job as the strange stranger, evoking some of the poetry that is in the Williams script. Marian Seldes does a straightforward job as the secretary, but the secretary is not the important character she used to be. Ruth Ford is all right, I guess, as a cynic and gossip known as the Witch of Capri.

Tony Richardson was the director.

The Gnädiges Fräulein, his black comedy which deals with outcasts from society and the dualities of life-death and flesh-spirit, contains more than a little grotesque humor and many of his best touches. Throughout the play, bitterness and humor are woven into a single strand of dramatic irony. The Cocolooney bird is an image of a Key West Pelican. The play, written under the influence of "speed," is a Williams favorite.

JOSEPH ABELES STUDIO

Margaret Leighton, Williams' gallant friend, starred in *Gnädiges Fräulein* as a German singer-dancer fallen on evil days, forced to compete with Cocolooney birds for deserted fish left on wharves.

JOSEPH ABELES STUDIO

The Mutilated starred Margaret Leighton and Zoe Caldwell, and with Gnädiges Fräulein was presented as a double bill called Slapstick Tragedy.

> I think the mutilated will
> Be touched by hands that nearly heal,
> At night the agonized will feel
> A comfort that is nearly real.
> A miracle, a miracle!
> A comfort that is nearly real.

JOSEPH ABELES STUDIO

BROADWAY POSTSCRIPT

Tripping on the Light Fantastic

IN ASSESSING two new Tennessee Williams works, it is not enough simply to dismiss them as misbegotten failures. Rather, one is inclined to view the double bill grouped under the title (Slapstick Tragedy) as a manifestation of a rightly celebrated playwright's latest creative impulse.

The first of the two playlets, The Mutilated, appears to be a naked plea for compassion in the tough, degraded society of sailors and whores in 1937 New Orleans. In it the playwright counterpoints the true Christian spirit and a cruelly selfish materialism. The Christopher Flanders-Mrs. Goforth axis of The Milk Train Doesn't Stop Here Anymore is here altered by making the compassionate Trinket Dugan the character with the wealth, and the tenacious Celeste Delacroix Griffin the character who is down and out.

Unfortunately, in the Broadway production the play emerges as a series of petty quarrels and a too shallow display of end results, as if the playwright had either become impatient with the task of exploring the deeper motives for his characters' actions, or had been restricted by the shortness of the one-act-play form. While there are recognizable flashes of Williams's unique talent, the play seems a mere dramatic exercise. Its exposition is thrust at us bluntly, and its brief events seem out of key with the formal Christmas Carol that bridges them.

The actresses, too, suffer from the play's abruptness, which allows little subtlety. As Celeste, Kate Reid pushes a blatantly realistic rather than a poetically moving vulgarity at us. And Margaret Leighton, who glowingly achieves the pathos of the breast-amputee, Trinket, has no chance to show us the gradual transition from resentment to compassion that constitutes the play's most important action.

The second piece, Gnadige Fraulëin, is a more interesting piece of theater. In front of Ming Cho Lee's beautifully ramshackle setting of a Florida Key boarding house, euphemistically known as "the big dormitory," we meet several bizarre characters. There is Polly, the local society columnist, audaciously and magnificently performed by Zoe Caldwell. Miss Caldwell is a superb mixture of music hall, camp, and satirical dignity as she informs the audience, "I did the southernmost write-up of the southernmost gangbang, and called it 'multiple nuptials.'" There is Molly the ruthless boarding-house proprietress, "a

vulgar, slovenly bitch with social pretensions" played by Kate Reid in droll clownish style. And there is the down-on-her-luck ex-European vaudevillian and B-girl, portrayed by Margaret Leighton. Miss Leighton gives it a good try, but sprinting after discarded fish is not really her cup of tea. Finally there is the grotesque cocaloony bird, nicely acted by Art Ostrin in Noel Taylor's inspired costume that makes him resemble nothing so much as a gleefully vicious drama critic in witty pursuit of some presumptuous antagonist.

One is merrily entertained by much of the goings-on, and admires director Alan Schneider's searchings for style. Above all one appreciates Mr. Williams's originality of conception, particularly when it is occasionally graced with such penetrating Tennesseeisms as "The dark angel has a duplicate key to the big dormitory." However, as in the late Sean O'Casey's Cock-a-Doodle Dandy, the fantastic quality of the proceedings often appears too much of a theatrical stunt.

Nevertheless, of the two playlets, it is certainly the more effective. Since even with the best material Broadway is notoriously inhospitable to any bill of unrelated short plays, it would be silly to take the official failure of Slapstick Tragedy, which closed after only seven performances, as a sign of Mr. Williams's waning talent. Rather it is simply a mistake in judgment (much as was Edward Albee's Malcolm) and should not prejudice anyone about the potential quality of our most distinguished living playwright's future work.
—HENRY HEWES.

Designer Taylor's "cocaloony bird"

Tennessee Williams talks about his play
"In The Bar of a Tokyo Hotel"

(During rehearsals, Mr. Williams wrote this letter to his cast.)

Please read to the company the following two paragraphs
of this letter, as I think it may clarify for them the intention
of the play, its "Meaning".

It is about the usually early and peculiarly humiliating
doom of the artist. He has made, in the beginning of his vocation,
an almost total commitment of himself to his work. As Mark
truthfully says, the intensity of the work, the unremitting
challenges and demands that it makes to him and of him (in most
cases daily) leave so little of him after the working hours
that simple, comfortable <u>being</u> is impossible for him. In some
cases, that may be familiar to us, he is afraid to answer a
ringing phone, afraid of a waiter in a restaurant, afraid of
his breath and his heart-beat. He is afraid of cutlery on a
table. He is afraid of his small dog's attitude toward him.

In the beginning, in his youth, the health of his
body enabled him to do his work and cope with his life outside
it. He is reticent, but he usually has a strong sexual drive.
The same fierce need that he brings to his work, he will bring
to finding for himself a wife or a lover. For a few years
this wife or lover will accept, or appear to accept, his
primary commitment to his work. Then the wife or lover will
reasonably resent being so constantly in second place, and
will pay him back by promiscuities, sometimes as ravenous
as Miriam's. His youth passes. The health of his body fails him.
Then the work increases its demand from most of him to practically all of him. At last it seems to him like an impotent
attempt at making love. At that point, he is sentenced to
death, and as death approaches, he hasn't the comfort of
feeling with any conviction that any of his work has had any
essential value. The wife or lover is repelled by his shattered
condition and is willing to be with him as little a time as
possible. Somewhere in her or him there remains, unconsciously,
a love for him that can only be expressed in her or his feeling
when the artist is dead.

I hope I've said something helpful.

Tennessee

Anne Meacham and Donald Madden couldn't save *In a Bar in a Tokyo Hotel*. Critics found the play and the relationships difficult to follow. It marked a low point in Williams' career.

JOSEPH ABELES STUDIO

Boom, the filmed version of *Milk Train*, starred the Richard Burtons with Noël Coward playing the Witch of Capri role created by Mildred Dunnock on Broadway. Playwright William Inge considered *Boom* the best film script he'd ever read.

for Tenn
just with gratitude
that he lives and
works —
Bill Inge

Williams was instrumental in helping William Inge at the outset of his career. Margo Jones produced *Farther Off from Heaven,* an early version of *Come Back, Little Sheba,* and Audrey Wood became Inge's agent. Williams, always a wary competitor, wrote a touching tribute to the gentle playwright at the time of his tragic death. Inge dedicated *Dark at the Top of the Stairs* to Williams.

Williams was baptized a Roman Catholic on January 6, 1969 (The Feast of the Epiphany) in the church of St. Mary Star of the Sea in Key West, Florida, saying, "I wanted my goodness back." One of his sponsors was his brother Dakin, whom Williams considers the greatest living eccentric in the States.

Williams was dining with Marion Vaccaro in Miami the following evening when the Miami *Herald* called and said, "We understand you're having a dinner party for Tennessee Williams." Marion said, "We're four people having ham and grits if you call that a dinner party. Mr. Williams is leaving for Rome in the morning; we think of it rather as the last supper."

DON PINDER, KEY WEST

New York Times

S, SUNDAY, JUNE 30, 1968

WILLIAMS TELLS BROTHER HE'S FINE

Playwright Phones to Allay Fears, but Doesn't Appear

By PAUL HOFMANN

Tennessee Williams surfaced in New York long enough yesterday to telephone his brother in Collinsville, Ill., and assure him he was alive and well.

W. Dakin Williams, the playwright's brother, who is a lawyer, said, "He must have had a bad scare."

The playwright's brother disclosed on Friday that he had received a note last week, dated June 22, in which Mr. Williams expressed fear for his life. Mr. Williams could not be reached in his West Side apartment here, or elsewhere, on Friday.

"My brother is in New York, but not in his apartment," the Collinsville lawyer said. "He asked me to tell mother not to worry."

But Mrs. Edwina Williams, the playwright's 86-year-old mother, hadn't been worrying anyway. At her St. Louis home earlier yesterday, Mrs. Williams chuckled and said: "My son has done such things before." She said she had not heard directly from him recently, but added that she was not upset over his apparent disappearance.

The playwright's secretary and companion, Bill Glavin, was quoted by an acquaintance yesterday as having explained in a telephone conversation earlier in the day that the reports about death threats against Mr. Williams and his disappearance had all been a "ghastly mistake."

'Trip to Cuba Planned?

Trip to Cuba Planned?

The source quoted Mr. Glavin as saying that he and Mr. Williams were planning to travel to Florida, and later possibly to Cuba. The playwright had stayed on in Key West, Fla., on earlier occasions. Mr. Glavin could not be reached later yesterday. "Bill has moved out," a man answering his telephone said.

The Police Department said that "We have no alarm for Mr. Williams out." On Friday, detectives assigned to investigate the case reported that the playwright had moved from his two-bedroom apartment on the 33d floor of 15 West 72d Street, without leaving a new address. The police said Mr. Williams had not made any complaint that his life was threatened.

The message, according to Mr. Williams's brother, was in the playwright's handwriting and read in part: "If anything of a violent nature happens to me, ending my life abruptly, it will not be a case of suicide, as it would be made to appear.

"I am not happy, it is true, in a net of con men, but I am hard at work, which is my love, you know."

Fear Appears Gone

The Collinsville lawyer said he had the impression from the telephone talk with his brother that Mr. Williams was no longer afraid his life was in danger. "He never acted that way before," the 54-year-old writer's brother remarked. He indicated he thought Mr. Williams would leave New York soon.

The playwright had been quite disturbed, his brother said, to learn that detectives, reporters and cameramen were "swarming all over New York" looking for him. The lawyer said he had counseled his brother to call The New York Times to set at rest any concern about his well-being. However, no such call had been received up to last night.

Friends of Mr. Williams recalled that even under ordinary circumstances it often was difficult to reach the playwright. He frequently ignored telephone calls gathered by his answering service and failed to respond to other messages, these sources said.

In an interview on Friday, Mr. Williams's brother said that the playwright had been "depressed" by unfavorable reviews of his play "The Seven Descents of Myrtle" and of "Boom!" a film based on his play "The Milk Train Doesn't Stop Here Anymore."

149

Tennessee Williams Expresses Fear for Life in Note to Brother

By MURRAY SCHUMACH

Tennessee Williams has sent a hand-written note to his brother expressing fear that he may be murdered.

The message, scribbled on the stationery of a New York restaurant, was dated June 22 and was received by W. Dakin Williams, a lawyer, last Wednesday, at his home in Collinsville, Ill.

The note, which Mr. Williams said was undoubtedly in his brother's handwriting, said:

"If anything of a violent nature happens to me, ending my life abruptly, it will not be a case of suicide, as it would be made to appear.

"I am not happy, it is true, in a net of con men, but I am hard at work, which is my love, you know."

New York City detectives assigned to look into the case learned that the playwright has moved from his two-bedroom apartment on the 33d floor of 15 West 72d Street. His lease of the $500 apartment expires tomorrow and Mr. Williams had reported his intention of moving four months ago.

The police said they were unable to learn his new address and would continue to investigate. They noted that he had not made any complaint to them of any threat against his life.

Dakin Williams, reached by telephone, said the note had been written in ink, except for a headline in pencil, saying, "Melodramatic But True." It was on stationery of L'Escargot Restaurant, 987 Third Avenue, between 58th and 59th Streets.

"I feel there must be some substance in this," Mr. Williams said. "He's not the sort of person who would write such a note. It's the first time anything like this has ever happened. I believe he's in quite imminent danger. I'm inclined to think he's picked up and gone into hiding. I put the story out mainly to prevent anything happening to him."

The 54-year-old playwright, whose successes include "The Glass Menagerie," "A Streetcar Named Desire," "Summer and Smoke," "The Rose Tattoo" and "Cat on a Hot Tin Roof," had been depressed, his brother said, by unfavorable reviews of his play "The Seven Descents of Myrtle" and of "Boom!", a film based on his play "The Milk Train Doesn't Stop Here Anymore."

Dakin Williams added that his brother was also "being pressured by some people, including one person who wants to do the screen version of 'One Arm,'" a short story. He declined to name the person.

The playwright's lawyer, Alan Schwartz, of Greenbaum, Wolff & Ernst, tried to reach his client by telegram and telephone. He had received no acknowledgement as of last night.

Friends of the writer noted that even under ordinary conditions, Mr. Williams often ignored telephone messages gathered by his answering service until they had piled up. Even then, they said, sometimes he ignored them all, answered all or just answered those he wished.

"He is quite unpredictable in such matters," a man who has known him for some years said.

The playwright's 86-year-old mother, Edwina, who lives in St. Louis, was described by Dakin Williams as "very upset."

New York Times

Playwright hospitalized

ST. LOUIS (AP) — Tennessee Williams' brother says the playwright has been in a hospital since Sept. 21 for treatment of the effects of long use of a sleeping pill.

The brother, Dakin Williams, an attorney of Collinsville, Ill., said Williams fell ill during a visit with ther mother, Mrs. Edwina Dakin Williams, in suburban Clayton.

He added that the playwright, 55, would stay in Barnes Hospital indefinitely but planned to attend the opening of his play "Camino Real" in New York Jan. 8.

Oct 3/69

This newspaper clipping gave little hint of the behind-the-scenes drama which unfolded at the Barnes Hospital in St. Louis. Williams' first words upon awakening from a knockout injection were: "Where Am I? The Plaza?", a remark he considers one of Dakin's inventions.

WALTER HAMPDEN MEMORIAL LIBRARY AT THE PLAYERS CLUB

The New York Times

Letters to the Editor

Amphetamines: What They're For and What They're Not For

To the Editor:

The article entitled "Amphetamine and Accidental Addicts," which accompanied your Dec. 4 news story on the use of amphetamines, contains some statements that are incomplete and others that are misleading. Lest some patients who are taking the medication for proper indication and in proper amounts be unsettled by these opinions, I should like to record a responsible dissent.

It is true that amphetamine is not always effective as an antidepressant. In fact, it is seldom effective. Usually the antidepression effect is achieved only with doses so high that they produce mental and physical disturbance.

However, when it is effective in low doses, its side effects are so much less frequent and less dangerous than those of the more potent, newer antidepressants, that in my opinion it should be considered the drug of choice. Some patients cannot tolerate the newer drugs at all, so that one must necessarily fall back upon amphetamines or similarly acting substances when and if they are helpful.

It has indeed been said by some medical authorities that amphetamine is indicated only for narcolepsy and hyperkinetic behavior disorders. However, I don't know how widely that opinion is held, and I disagree with it.

Amphetamine is useful to overcome the excessive and unwelcome soporific effects of other medications such as some tricyclic antidepressants, some phenothiazine tranquilizers and even antihistamine drugs. It is useful to overcome compulsive sleepiness which is psychogenic rather than narcoleptic.

It is useful to overcome disabling neurotic inertia which is not accompanied by severe depression. The proper treatment of depression requires a regimen involving one or more modalities of treatment and the use of one or more chemical agents. In such a regimen, amphetamine may occasionally play an important role.

It is true that the protracted use of amphetamine in excessive doses may lead to psychosis, but the short-term use of the newer antidepressants in excessive doses is even more likely to induce psychosis or mania. One-time use of amphetamine in normal doses is most unlikely to elicit assaultive behavior or delusions of omnipotence.

There are few substances in the

Ed Fisher

pharmacopocia, and few medical procedures in general, that do not lend themselves to abuse and that are without some degree of risk. Moreover, addictive personalities can establish addictions to the most innocent substances, including food, milk and water, to the point of serious damage sometimes, and even death.

Obviously, the only safeguard the patient has is the integrity and sound judgment of his physician, who must at every point in his work carefully weigh reward against risk. To refuse to employ an indicated procedure when the reward-risk ratio is high is no less reprehensible than it is to use it when that ratio is low. The element of judgment can never be eliminated from the practice of medicine.

MORTIMER OSTOW, M.D.
New York, Dec. 5, 1972

●

To the Editor:

Boyce Rensberger's Dec. 4 news story on the use of amphetamines by "famous patients" affected me the same way the Black Sox scandal of years past affected the little boy who pleaded: "Say it ain't so, Joe."

Made desperate by vanity and thirsting for the social and material rewards that thanks to twentieth-century technologies the communications industry can overnight make possible, there is a mad scramble for instant fame. Along with instant coffee, instant soup, why not instant greatness? Thus, creative artists, politicians, top-flight executives and wealthy nonentities resort to the drug-

tipped hypodermic as standard equipment on their way up the success ladder.

I never imagined that a more civilized ethic could be found at the race track. Doped horses, no matter how outstanding their performance, are at once disqualified, the purses forfeited, the trainer often ruled off the turf for life and the owner, though at times innocent, no longer permitted his racing colors. No Oscars or high office for them.

And that is as it should be. If the poor horse is made to do it on its own, ought we to expect less of humans?

IRVING CAESAR
New York, Dec. 4, 1972

●

To the Editor:

In the long piece about Dr. Max Jacobson [Dec. 4] I have been singled out among the many persons mentioned as patients of his—and in a manner which is very embarassing and damaging to my character.

It is true that for two or three years in the late sixties I went to Dr. Jacobson for treatment of a deep depression. But it is totally untrue that I was ever "thrown out" of the office for "boozing it up" in the waiting room. Whoever dispensed this bit of low-comedy invention should be required to retract it.

I would say that the entire matter of listing the doctor's patients is an invasion of privacy of a highly damaging nature; if their names came from the doctor's office it is surely a breach of medical ethics.

I have not seen the doctor nor been in his office since the spring of '69. During the sixties I drank heavily but I never behaved like a "drunken bum," as I am depicted in your article.

As for the doctor himself, I am inclined to believe that he was a brilliant experimenter but that in certain cases, including mine, the experiments—perhaps like all medical experiments—happened to involve a good deal of hazard.

I think his motives are humanitarian. I can't believe that he himself issued the slanderous statement about me.

You have my word, if you will accept it, that the alleged incident did not occur.

TENNESSEE WILLIAMS
New York, Dec. 6, 1972

Back home in Key West, Williams made a swift return to health, and soon was his old self again.

WRIGHT LANGLEY, KEY WEST

Williams and Norman Mailer in New York at a benefit for The Peoples' Coalition for Peace and Justice where excerpts from Mailer's *Why Are We in Vietnam?* were performed. An amused Gore Vidal commented that it was the first time Williams realized that we were in Vietnam. Earlier, when Williams told Vidal that he slept all through the sixties, Vidal replied, "You didn't miss a thing."

UNITED PRESS INTERNATIONAL PHOTO

Tennessee as "Doc" in *Small Craft Warnings*. His first and only appearance in one of his own plays. Until he got his lines down, his ad-libs drove the cast to distraction.

WORLD WIDE PHOTO

Williams presented the Academy Award for the best screenplay to Paddy Chayefsky for *Hospital* at the 1972 awards in Hollywood, making an impressive entrance down a long flight of stairs. As his health returned, he made more and more public appearances and was soon completely engrossed in new work.

In New York with fellow playwright Edward Albee, considered by many Williams admirers to be the Crown Prince.

COLLECTION OF TENNESSEE WILLIAMS
ACADEMY OF MOTION PICTURE ARTS AND SCIENCES

Tennesse Williams

'I've never faked it'

by Arthur Bell

We're in a rehearsal hall in the Irish Institute. It's the last day of casting for "Small Craft Warnings" and there are still three male roles to fill. One is that of a boozed-up stud and Tennessee Williams wants to see that the role is filled right, seeing as how he wrote the play. The room we're in is about as Irish as Roman Polanski but it doesn't matter: there's plenty of room for an actor to do his Stanley Kowalski bit to an audience, which in addition to Tennessee includes director Bill Hunt, leading lady Helena Carroll, and two producers.

Tennessee is jubilant. "Actors always thrill me when they're good," he says, "they always lift a script beyond its written limits." And despite the fact that his face is over-ripe with red cor-puscles, he looks good too, better than he has in a long time, and he's full of the devil and filled with beautiful words for the actors who file in, one at a time, to read.

The first on call is a burly hunk named Brad Sullivan. He's got Brando karma and a stud aura, chunky arms, a soupcon of a beer belly, he's wearing a McBurney sweatshirt, scissored off at the armpits, which helps matters. Tennessee takes off his glasses and stares at him, good and hard. Sullivan begins from the script. "I'll go in the gents, and he'll follow me in there for a look at Junior. Then I'll have him hooked." He's playing it out of the side of his mouth, lots of long pauses, punchdrunk. Tennessee likes what he sees and he signals the director and Bill Hunt asks Sullivan to do it again. "Soften it a little bit," he says, "don't make it so nasty and strong." It works better the second time. "He's very good and he could be wonderful," says Tennessee after Sullivan has left the room. "He wasn't vicious and he keeps the poetry."

"The next boy is physically right," claims Hunt. "Wait till you see him." Physically right enters and eyes pop. Tennessee's face grows red with pleasure. "Mmmmm, you're right." He pushes his glasses to his head. The actor reads the speech, soft, an interpretation more Blanche Du Bois than Stanley Kowalski. "I've never done a lick of work in my life and I never plan to, not as long as Junior keeps batting on the home team."

"Very beautiful. Beautiful. Superb reading. Thank you very much. You're beautiful," glows Tennessee.

"You are too, Mr. Williams," says the actor, as he's guided out of the room. There is a two-minute pause. Finally. "Do you think he can act?" from Helena Carroll. Bill Hunt answers. "We can probably get something out of him," and Tennessee rolls his eyes.

The next actor plays it from the edge of his seat. It's a method reading with stomach-scratching but the scratching produces blood and Hunt tells him that he's too into it and suggests that he get further away from the part. Tennessee is making notes in his yellow pad and tells the actor he's beautiful, but the actor looks sad and isn't convinced.

The audition continues. One young man who looks like he's spent the last 20 years of his life lifting weights tells Tennessee "I do it all different ways. Any way you want. I'm an actor." Another man expounds on what he believes to be the motivation of the character: "He is a man who has found himself dead and doesn't like it," and Tennessee answers with "the only problem there is if you play that he's dead, the audience will be dead, and they won't like it."

Finally, Brad Sullivan is asked to return. After another reading and several "you're beautifuls" Sullivan explains that in his

Voice: Fred W. McDarrah
TENNESSEE WILLIAMS

opinion the character of the stud is not a bad guy, he's sort of humorous, and that's how he played it. "Someone told me once," says Sullivan, "that a woman when she's bad is bad through and through, but a bad man always has a redeeming quality." Tennessee honey oozes, "I remember a man in Oklahoma who didn't have one redeeming quality." It looks as though Brad Sullivan has the part.

* * *

154

Elizabeth Ashley was a brilliant Maggie in the American Shakespeare Theatre's revival of *Cat on a Hot Tin Roof*. If Williams thinks she's slightly inclined to excess, he also wishes she'd take better care of herself "as befits the new Queen of Broadway."

AMERICAN SHAKESPEARE THEATRE

At the twentieth anniversary of *The Glass Menagerie*, Williams celebrates the first of a dozen revivals of his work which would see as many as four productions during a single Broadway season. He confesses to falling asleep during *The Glass Menagerie* . . . until the entrance of The Gentleman Caller.

JOSEPH ABELES STUDIO

Williams considers Irene Worth, who received a Tony award for her brilliant performance as the Princess in the New York revival of *Sweet Bird of Youth,* to be possibly the greatest living actress of the English-speaking theater.

COURTESY OF DAVID POWERS

"A scene between Michael Moriarty (The Gentleman Caller) and Katherine Hepburn (Amanda Wingfield) from David Susskind's ABC presentation of *The Glass Menagerie* for which the talented young actor won a TONY award.

COURTESY OF ABC TELEVISION

Williams, his agent Bill Barnes, and Actress Faye Dunaway discussing her role of Blanche in the West Coast revival of *A Streetcar Named Desire* in Los Angeles.

COURTESY OF BILL BARNES

It is the Cathedral Church's privilege to present one of the first four medals struck in commemoration of the completion of its first century to

TENNESSEE WILLIAMS

foremost dramatist of our day, whose compassion for the suffering of others has served to increase the sensitivity of an insensitive age, and replace stones with human hearts.

The President,
the Governors
and the
Literary Committee of
The National Arts Club
15 Gramercy Park South
New York City
request the pleasure
of your company at

The Eighth Annual
Literary Award Dinner
honoring
Mr Tennessee Williams

Thursday, February 20, 1975

Reception at six-thirty
Dinner at seven-thirty
Festive Dress
rsvp

In Key West, Williams was made an honorary Conch (Key West native) by Monroe County Mayor Gerald Staundberg at a 1970 birthday party tended him at the Pier House by owner David Wolkowsky. One of Key West's most attractive shops is named The Glass Menagerie and a restaurant is called The Rose Tattoo.

WRIGHT LANGLEY, KEY WEST

Suddenly Last Summer was in final rehearsal at the' Greene Street Theater in Key West during April of 1976 when Williams drove up and delivered seven new lines of dialogue complete with stage directions to the startled cast with the notation "suggest this to make it more fluid." The new ending of the play has Mrs. Venable collapsing on stage rather than offstage. Williams dedicated the production to his friend the late Jo Mielziner, who had designed nine productions for him. Following the performance, an enthusiastic Williams led the applause saying, "I'll give them anything. I thought, for Key West, after all those revolting productions, to see a vigorous, semi-professional production—it's marvelous."

Greene Street Theatre

presents

"SUDDENLY LAST SUMMER"

by

Tennessee Williams

Directed by
WILLIAM PROSSER

Produced by
JOHN W. DRURY, RODERICK BROWN, and PETER PELL

CAST

Mrs. Venable ....Janice White
Dr. Cukrowicz..........................Jay Drury
Miss Foxhill........................Diane Kambos
Mrs. Holly ....Betty Smith
George Holly ....Gordon Mackey
Catharine Holly.....................Roxana Stuart
Sister Felicity ....Rita Buckner

"I would like this production of **Suddenly Last Summer** to serve as a tribute to the memory of Jo Mielziner, my dear friend and designer of several of my best plays."

— *Tennessee Williams*

Tennessee with Ruth Brinkmann in Vienna during the World Premiere of *The Red Devil Battery Sign*.

"At the World Premiere one will be able to ask oneself how an important work by one of the most important dramatists of our time could be so deeply misunderstood that he had to flee with his play to a foreign country. But perhaps one will heed him and be able to understand him from Vienna."

—Karin Kathrein
Die Presse

Another Vienna Reviewer (Beer) would claim that New York producers could not stomach the phantasmagoric part of the play and tried to have Williams retract it. Williams retracted the entire play instead and reworked it for its opening in the intimate English Theatre of Vienna where it played to capacity houses during the limited engagement.

The Vieux Carré in New Orleans became Williams' spiritual home in the winter of 1938, and it provided him with an immense amount of raw material, an inexhaustible fund of experience from which he continues to draw. Pictured during the recent New York production of *Vieux Carré* are (l-r) Richard Atfiere, Sylvia Sydney, Iris Whitney and Olive Deering.

JOSEPH ABELES STUDIO

Williams chats with the Modern American Primitive painter Henry Faulkner (whom Williams collects) as artist William Hargrove looks on in the Jane Bowles Summer House in Key West. The building sports an overhead fan, electric lights and has the name TOM cut into the decorations near the bottom. Faulkner includes one painting in every annual exhibition of his work entitled "Garden for Tennessee Williams."

COLLECTION OF HENRY FAULKNER

Miss Edwina on one of her more recent visits to her son's Key West home. She is in her nineties now; he remains concerned about her health and visits her frequently. Through the years since his father's death in 1957, Tennessee has come to think of him as a terribly unhappy man who had misunderstood his family, but a totally honest man who had lived life on his own terms, which were hard terms for his family.

DON PINDER, KEY WEST

Williams considers his care of his sister Rose to be one of the best things he's done with his life. He often entertains her at the Plaza in New York, and recently she made an extended visit to Key West. As bittersweet as her visits are, he hopes one day she can live with a companion in the Coconut Grove home he purchased for her years ago. He lavishes attention and gifts on her; their affection for each other remains the deepest in their lives.

COLLECTION OF TENNESSEE WILLIAMS

Tennessee relishes his brother Dakin's political career. Their paternal grandfather spent a fortune running unsuccessfully for governor of Tennessee. Dakin once challenged Adlai Stevenson III to a nude centerfold contest in *Cosmopolitan* magazine, and in Chicago's city hall he once performed a rite of exorcism. Following a period of estrangement, a reconciliation is in progress. Tennessee endorses Dakin in his current campaign for the governorship of Illinois because "He's always been good to our mother."

WORLD WIDE PHOTO

Tennessee signs his name on a door of the Humanities Research Center at the University of Texas in Austin during a visit there to inspect their collection of his manuscripts and papers. Years ago, he came up to Miami from his Duncan Street home in Key West to accept a Muse Award which hailed him as "Florida's Most Outstanding Playwright." He later observed somewhat dryly that he'd rather be known as "Duncan Street's Most Promising Playwright."

Bibliography
and Awards

PLAYS:

BATTLE OF ANGELS
STAIRS TO THE ROOF
THE GLASS MENAGERIE
YOU TOUCHED ME (IN COLLABORATION WITH DONALD WINDHAM)
A STREETCAR NAMED DESIRE
SUMMER AND SMOKE
THE ECCENTRICITIES OF A NIGHTINGALE
THE ROSE TATTOO
CAMINO REAL
CAT ON A HOT TIN ROOF
ORPHEUS DESCENDING
GARDEN DISTRICT: SOMETHING UNSPOKEN & SUDDENLY LAST SUMMER
SWEET BIRD OF YOUTH
PERIOD OF ADJUSTMENT
THE MILK TRAIN DOESN'T STOP HERE ANYMORE
THE NIGHT OF THE IGUANA
SLAPSTICK TRAGEDY: THE MUTILATED & THE GNÄDIGES FRÄULEIN
KINGDOM OF EARTH
THE SEVEN DESCENTS OF MYRTLE
THE TWO-CHARACTER PLAY
IN THE BAR OF A TOKYO HOTEL
SMALL CRAFT WARNINGS
OUT CRY
THE RED DEVIL BATTERY SIGN
VIEUX CARRÉ

SHORT PLAYS:

27 WAGONS FULL OF COTTON
THE PURIFICATION
THE LADY OF LARKSPUR LOTION
THE LAST OF MY SOLID GOLD WATCHES
PORTRAIT OF A MADONNA
AUTO-DA-FE
LORD BYRON'S LOVE LETTER

The Strangest Kind of Romance
The Long Goodbye
Hello from Bertha
This Property is Condemned
Talk to Me Like the Rain
I Rise in Flame, Cried the Phoenix
I Can't Imagine Tomorrow
Confessional
The Frosted Glass Coffin
A Perfect Analysis Given by a Parrot
At Liberty
The Enemy: Time
The Dark Room
10 Blocks on the Camino Real
The Case of the Crushed Petunias
The Unsatisfactory Supper
Moony's Kid Don't Cry
Demolition Downtown
Life-Boat Drill

ORIGINAL SCREENPLAY:

Baby Doll

TELEVISION PLAYS:

The Migrants (with Lanford Wilson)
Stopped Rocking

POETRY:

In the Winter of Cities
Androgyne, Mon Amour

PROSE:

One Arm (Stories)
The Roman Spring of Mrs. Stone (Novella)
Hard Candy (Stories)
The Knightly Quest (Novella and Stories)
Eight Mortal Ladies Possessed (Stories)
Moise and the World of Reason (Novel)
Memoirs (Autobiography)

AWARDS:

2 Rockefeller Fellowships
Grant from the Institute of Arts & Letters
New York Drama Critics' Circle Award for THE GLASS MENAGERIE (1945)

THE SIDNEY HOWARD MEMORIAL AWARD FOR THE GLASS MENAGERIE (1945)

NEW YORK DRAMA CRITICS' CIRCLE AWARD FOR A STREETCAR NAMED DESIRE (1948)

THE DONALDSON AWARD FOR A STREETCAR NAMED DESIRE (1948)

THE PULITZER PRIZE FOR A STREETCAR NAMED DESIRE (1948)

THE NEW YORK DRAMA CRITICS' CIRCLE AWARD FOR CAT ON A HOT TIN ROOF (1955)

THE PULITZER PRIZE FOR CAT ON A HOT TIN ROOF (1955)

THE NEW YORK DRAMA CRITICS' CIRCLE AWARD FOR NIGHT OF THE IGUANA (1962)

BRANDEIS UNIVERSITY CREATIVE ARTS AWARD (1965)

GOLD MEDAL FOR DRAMA BY THE AMERICAN ACADEMY OF ARTS & LETTERS
    AND THE NATIONAL INSTITUTE OF ARTS & LETTERS (1969)

DOCTOR OF HUMANITIES, UNIVERSITY OF MISSOURI (1969)

NATIONAL THEATRE CONFERENCE ANNUAL AWARD (1972)

DOCTOR OF LITERATURE, HONORIS CAUSA (1972) UNIVERSITY OF HARTFORD, CONNECTICUT

CENTENNIAL MEDAL OF THE CATHEDRAL CHURCH OF ST. JOHN THE DIVINE (1973)

ENTERTAINMENT HALL OF FAME AWARD (1974)

MEDAL OF HONOR FOR LITERATURE BY NATIONAL ARTS CLUB (1975)

Tennessee Williams Fine Arts Center
Florida Keys Community College
Dr. John Sylvester Smith, President

GROUND BREAKING/DEDICATION
TENNESSEE WILLIAMS
FINE ARTS CENTER
FLORIDA KEYS COMMUNITY COLLEGE
DECEMBER 11, 1977
THREE O'CLOCK
KEY WEST, FLORIDA

Index

En Avant!

Some productions of Tennessee Williams' plays during 1972–1977.